nothing in LIFE STARTS until YOU START

50 Principles For Becoming Extraordinary and Achieving More Success

MIKE DRIGGERS

Copyright © 2016 IME publishing group

ALL RIGHTS RESERVED no part of this book or its associated ancillary materials may be reproduced or transmitted in any form or by any means, electronic or mechanical, including photocopying, recording, or by any information of storage or retrieval system without the permission from the publisher.

PUBLISHED BY IME Publishing Group

DISCLAIMER AND/OR LEGAL NOTICES
While all attempts have been made to verify the information provided in this book and its ancillary materials, neither the author or the publisher assume any responsibility for errors, inaccuracies or omissions and is not responsible for any financial loss by consumer in any manner. Any slights of people or organizations are unintentional. If advice concerning legal, financial, accounting or related matters is needed, the service of a qualified professional should be sought. This book and its associated axillary materials, including verbal and written training, is not intended for use as a source of legal, financial or accounting advice. You should be aware of the various laws governing business transactions or other business practices in your particular geographical location.

EARNINGS AND INCOME DISCLAIMER
With respect to the reliability, accuracy, timeliness, usefulness, adequacy, completeness, and/or suitability of information provided in the book, Mike Driggers and IME Publishing Group its Partners Associates Affiliates Consultants and/or presenters make no warranties guarantees representations or claims of any kind. Readers results will vary depending on a number of factors. Any and all claims or representations as to income earnings are not to be considered and average earnings. Testimonials are not representative. This book and all products and services are for education and informational purposes only. Use caution and see the advice of qualified professionals. Check with your accountant, attorney or professional adviser before acting on this or any information. You agreed that Mike Driggers and IME Publishing Group is not responsible for the success or failure of your personal, business, health or financial decisions relating to any information presented by Mike Driggers and IME Publishing Group or Company products/services. Earnings potentials is entirely dependent on the efforts, skills and application of the individual person.

Any examples, stories, references, or case studies are for illustrative purposes only and should not be interpreted as testimonies and/or examples of what reader and/or consumers are generally expected from the information. No representation in any part of this information, materials and/or seminar trainings are guarantees or promises for actual performance. Any statements, strategies, concepts, techniques, exercises and ideas in the information materials and/or seminar training offered are simply opinion or experience, and thus should not be misinterpreted as promises, typical results or guarantees (expressed or implied). The author and the publisher (Mike Driggers, IME Publishing Group (IME) or any IME Representatives) Shall in no way, under any circumstances be held liable to any party (or third-party) for any direct, indirect, punitive, special, incidental or other consequential damages arising directly or indirectly from any use of books, materials and or seminar trainings, which is provided "as is," and without warranties

Mike Driggers / IME Publishing Group
www.SuccessWithMikeDriggers.com
www.IMEPublishingGroup.com

IME Publishing Group/ Mike Driggers —1st ed.
ISBN: - 978-0-9973034-3-8

PRINTED IN THE UNITED STATES OF AMERICA

WHAT OTHERS ARE SAYING ABOUT MIKE DRIGGERS AND HIS STRATEGIES

Recommend To All Leaders – Great Insights!
— **Daniel Eugene** "Rudy" Ruettiger, Played football for University of Notre Dame and In 1993, TRISTAR Productions immortalized his life story with the blockbuster film, "RUDY"

Mike Driggers principles offer a fresh and timely perspective that will ignite your soul and put fuel on your internal fire to go out and be the best you can be in your personal and professional life. — **Jill Lublin**, CEO, PublicityCrashCourse.com, International Speaker & 4x Best selling Author

Whether you're a seasoned business leader, a recent graduate just starting your career or an entrepreneur, Mike Driggers principles and approach apply across all Industries and disciplines. Mike's attitude is inspiring and he is an outstanding mentor. — **Jonathan Atkinson**, Criminal Investigator Santa Clara County District Attorney's Office

Mike's ideologies to achieving everything you ever wanted in business and in Life gives you a step-by-step blueprint that will make you strive harder and push further than you ever have. — **Sonia Hinojo**, Air Liquid Sales and Marketing Manager

Mike's practical ways to becoming a high achiever in business and in your personal life through his simple to use principles are a must-have and I highly recommend you learn them now. — **Greg Kite**, Former NBA Player for the Boston Celtics & Executive Field Chairman for Hegemon Group International

GREAT meeting today--as usual, terrific atmosphere for connecting, and a great tactics and strategy exercise led by Mike. — **David Hirata**, Theatrical Modern Magician

I really appreciate the high quality of biz coaching my group has from Mike Driggers! — **Ellen Vaughn Simonin**, Physical Therapist and Acupuncturist

The ideas presented by Mike Driggers offer an inspiration and exciting perspective that will change the course of how you succeed in business or life. — **Steve Jones**, 10 years Law Enforcement

Whether you're an executive at a fortune 500 company or an entrepreneur Mike Driggers solutions go far beyond traditional business practices. Any organization can put this to immediate use and achieve amazing results. — **Steve Aust,** Former NBA Player for the Los Angeles Lakers, Chairman Co-Founder of Agora Advantage

Mike Driggers strategies are remarkable and insightful. He provides an easy-to-understand blueprint that makes you want to jump ahead and implement his process immediately.
— **Belza López**, Housing Specialist for the City of Napa

Mike Driggers Concepts will become an invaluable tool in business and life for those who are on a pursuit of Excellence and Success. — **Gabriela Aguilera**, Orthodontic Treatment Coordinator

LET'S MAKE IT HAPPEN TODAY

Special **FREE** Bonus Gift For **YOU!**

To help you stand out from the crowd
FREE BONUS RESOURCE for you at;
www.letsmakeithappentoday.com/sp.html

Get your FREE Report And You'll Discover...

1. How to avoid being like the vast majority of people, having hundreds of projects started and never completed

2. How to choose and write Your goals effectively, how to write effective action plans and how to make sure you stick with your goals and never give up.

3. How to become remarkably effective by fulfilling your Goals and Start Living the Life of Your Dreams

www.letsmakeithappentoday.com/sp.html

Nothing In LIFE Starts Until YOU Start

"Share This Book"

Retail 24.95

Special Quantity Discounts

5-20 Books	21.95
21-99 Books	18.95
100-499 Books	15.95
500-999 Books	10.95
1,000 + Books	8.95

To Order Go To www.BookMikeToday.com

THE IDEAL PROFESSIONAL SPEAKER FOR YOUR NEXT EVENT!

Any organization that wants to develop and grow their business to become "extraordinary" needs to hire Mike for a keynote and / or workshop training!

TO CONTACT OR BOOK MIKE TO SPEAK:

IME Publishing Group

(866) 7BOOKME

(866) 726-6563

www.BookMikeToday.com

Info@SuccessWithMikeDriggers.com

DEDICATION

Many thanks and praises to GOD Almighty
who has guided me on the path that he has chosen for me.

This book is dedicated to my son Alex who is my driving spirit and
my greatest accomplishment in life.

My thanks go to my Mother and Father, who have always believed in
me and have encouraged me to reach for the stars.

A special thanks goes out to my sweetheart, Gaby Aguilera, who has
played a tremendous part in helping make this book a reality.
Also, greatthanks to James Malinchak who helped with the finer
details of the concepts. And special thanks to Ed Melliza photography.

Special thanks to all the great mentors, coaches and business partners

whose teachings have had a profound impact on my personal and
business life.

CONTENTS

A Message To You xv
Introduction xi
Principle 1 Taking the Initiative 1
Principle 2 Change is Not Your Enemy 3
Principle 3 Why You Are What You Think 5
Principle 4 Keep Your Mind Open to New Ideas 7
Principle 5 Life is How You Experience it 9
Principle 6 Why it's Never Too Late to Start Fresh 11
Principle 7 The Capacity for Acceptance 13
Principle 8 Finding Your True Happiness 15
Principle 9 The Impact of Positive Thinking 17
Principle 10 You Must Not Be Afraid to Make Mistakes ... 21
Principle 11 Finding Good Motivations 23
Principle 12 Why you should Dream Big 25
Principle 13 Follow your Passions 27
Principle 14 Thinking Outside the Box 29
Principle 15 Personal Growth 31
Principle 16 Become Mindful 33
Principle 17 Before You Start Something 35
Principle 18 Clear away the Stress 39
Principle 19 Form Clear Cut Goals 41
Principle 20 Using Strategic Planning to achieve Success ... 43
Principle 21 Develop a Strong Work Ethic 45
Principle 22 Getting into the Zone 47
Principle 23 Strengthen Your Willpower 49
Principle 24 Fostering Discipline 51
Principle 25 The Importance of Focus and Monotasking ... 53
Principle 26 Give Time to Nurture Yourself 55

Principle 27 You'll Always Need a Strong Support System 57
Principle 28 The Significance of Emotional Intelligence 59
Principle 29 Developing Professionalism 63
Principle 30 Developing Competence in Yourself and Others .. 65
Principle 31 Learn to Listen 69
Principle 32 Human Connections 71
Principle 33 Why You Should Live with Loving Kindness 73
Principle 34 Staying Humble 75
Principle 35 An Attitude for Happiness 77
Principle 36 Being Thankful 79
Principle 37 Why It's a Good Idea to be Frugal 81
Principle 38 The Secrets to Risk-Taking in Business 83
Principle 39 Develop Effective Time Management Skills 85
Principle 40 The Benefits of Exercise 87
Principle 41 Eating Healthy 89
Principle 42 Sleep 91
Principle 43 Why Spirituality Matters 93
Principle 44 The Strength of Affirmations 95
Principle 45 Choosing Love 97
Principle 46 How to Have a Lasting Relationship 99
Principle 47 Love Yourself 101
Principle 48 Being at Peace 105
Principle 49 Empowering the World 107
Principle 50 Live Life to the Fullest 109
One Last Message 111
About The Author 113

"TRUE SUCCESS IS NOT THE END DESTINATION, IT IS A MEASURE OF DOING THE COMMON THINGS UNCOMMONLY WELL ON THE JOURNEY TO SUCCESS."

A MESSAGE TO YOU!

Hi, I'm Mike Driggers, and I wanted to congratulate you on the wise decision to continue your education and the investment you just made in yourself..

I'm extremely proud of your decision to invest in you because you have literally done what most people will not do. I believe that this is the biggest reasons why people fail to achieve the results that they desire in their personal and professional lives.

Most people do not invest time or money into any type of continued education once they have finished schooling in order to learn new strategies that can create successful results. What's funny is that these are the same people that sit around complaining and blame society for their lack of success and it is never them. I am sure you are familiar with what I'm talking about. We all have either met or know someone who has this disease called excusitis. They us the "if it wasn't for" saying.

If it wasn't for the economy, president, location, my boss, I would have...

These are the type of people that always place blame on others issues. They would rather spend time focusing on why it can't be done than making a decision to take action and focus on why they can and what they need to do to make it happen.

However, this is why you will stand out from the rest. You are different because you have decided to take action by continu ing your education and investing in yourself. Because of this I have a incredible amount of respect for you.

One of my favorite quotes that illustrates my point is

> *"I am not a product of my circumstances.*
> *I am a product of my decisions."* — *Stephen Covey.*

It is the mindset that makes a difference in your outcome. Every action has a reaction and the decision you make whether positive or negative determines the outcome. Making the decision to invest in yourself always has the highest returns. In all the courses and books I have spent money on I have never looked at it as spent money I looked at it as I have invested in me just like you have with investing in you with this book.

I look at your decision as you want to be better and you have invested in yourself to do so. I believe your success will be in direct proportion to your continues personal development. I am in celebration for your decision not because you bought my book but because are continuing to develop YOU.

Why did I put these principles together in a book

Earlier in my career, I learned from different mentors in my life and these are a collection of different principles I have developed, perfected and applied in my life. So, I decided to pay it forward. I decided I would put them in a book. To give back and provide a tool for others like you to use in your future success.

In this book have I listed 50 simple, yet powerful principles that I believe will take you to a higher performance level in your business, sales, leadership and in your life. They are all individual principles that are organized in a manner that makes each independent of the others. You can read or do not need to read in a sequential order. You could just simply flip through to any principles that appeals to you or read them in order either way works.

Some principles will be new to you while others will be a reminder. Some you will easily be able to implement. While others may take little bit of extra effort. Some of these principles will Comfort you. While others will change your old paradigm. One thing is for certain, these principles will have you thinking and acting differently. I sincerely hope we can meet in person here in the near future. However, until then it is my great honor to meet you through the pages of this book.

> "IF AN INVISIBLE PERSON FOLLOWED YOU AROUND ALL DAY, WHAT WOULD THEY SEE?"

INTRODUCTION

Choosing empowerment and positivity, or negativity and unhappiness, is a decision that you're making every day, whether you realize it or not.

When I was younger I heard a Native American story that was passed down through it's culture of a man who explains his own constant struggle between positive, empowering, creative impulses and negative and self-destructive ones by telling his son that he has two wolves fighting in his heart -- a good wolf and a bad one.

The boy asks him which of the two will win the battle. The father replies, "Whichever one I feed."

It's very true. The feelings that we nurture and return to, time after time, are the ones which come to dominate our thoughts and actions, while the ones we turn away from fade away.

The exciting thing is, we have a choice. Although the two wolves both exist, we can choose which one of them we want to feed. That means, we choose which one will win.

You probably know people who feel sorry for themselves, who belittle others, who seem to get some kind of pleasure out of feeling miserable, who portray themselves as victims and reject the affections of anyone who doesn't offer constant sympathy. Often it seems to everybody but themselves that they actually have a whole lot going for them, but they're apt to be defensive if anyone should ever dare to point that out!

That's a classic example of what happens when you feed the bad wolf. You don't satisfy an appetite for any kind of feeling when you feed it - you only make it stronger. If you indulge negative feelings about yourself or other people, you strengthen them until they're very hard indeed to break away from.

The other side of the coin's what happens when you feed the GOOD wolf. If you know people who always seem to get a real kick out of life, who laugh a lot, have lots of friends and interests, and light up the room with energy and sparkle, who succeed in everything they turn their hand to and who always seem to have a lot of fun, you don't need ask which wolf THEY'RE feeding.

So, how DO you feed the good wolf, then? You give it what it most enjoys.

It has the most enormous appetite for feeling good, for having a positive self-image and strong self-esteem, for kindness, understanding, positive attitudes and healthy laughter. It feeds on self-respect, and tolerance for other people. It thrives on learning skills for the achievement of a purpose, and it loves the satisfaction of attaining worthwhile goals. It laps up happiness. Above all, it relishes enjoying life and sharing joy with others.

When was the last time you wanted to laugh aloud, or sing, or dance, or turn a somersault, just from the sheer delight of being alive? That state of mind is the one that feeds the good wolf best of all.

If YOUR good wolf's been going hungry, here are 50 principles for achieving extraordinary life and massive success, and it all starts from YOU. Look them over; give some thought to each of them; and adapt them to your own life.

> "TWO THINGS TO THINK ABOUT, YOU MISS ALL THE SHOTS YOU DON'T TAKE, AND THERE IS NO TRAFFIC ON THE FREEWAY OF GREATNESS?"

"GET COMFORTABLE WITH BEING UNCOMFORTABLE."

PRINCIPLE 1

TAKING THE INITIATIVE

Taking the initiative means being able to do your work and solve problems on your own. This means you can work with some level of independence. The ability to take the initiative is an important skill to learn in order to become successful and rise to the top quickly.

Showing a knack for taking the initiative is important in making decisive decisions even without supervision. It means that you are capable of filling in whenever or wherever needed and that you can go above and beyond your assigned task. This means that you can handle things when your boss is suddenly unavailable, you can find out things that you need to know without having to ask, and you can identify and grab hold of the opportunities that come your way. With initiative, you no longer just react to things as they happen; you are the one making things happen. With initiative, you can truly take control of life.

Develop initiative at work

If you want to develop initiative in the workplace, you need three things: knowledge, good instincts, and a lot of confidence. Remember that there is a big difference between taking the initiative and acting rashly. Don't make any decisions that you don't really understand yet, or don't go running to your boss to pitch a half-baked idea. Once you recognize an opportunity, make a study and ensure your plan or idea is solid. It would also be good to have some emotional sensibility when handling these matters. Read the room, so to speak, so that your initiative can be seen in the best possible light.

Initiative means taking action

Developing initiative means developing a mind set for taking action. Instead of being overly cautious and turning into a sitting duck during stressful or crisis situations, you can take on an active role and effectively do your part to help alleviate the situation. It also means being able to keep going despite setbacks and difficulties you may encounter. Having the initiative means being able to persist in your chosen task and continue to actively work when lesser people would just quit.

Initiative means taking control

Initiative also means taking control. When you imbibe the idea of taking initiative even within your life, you stop just waiting for things to happen, you make it happen. You don't just wait for better opportunities or a promotion, you actively seek them out or present yourself for a position that you know you're qualified for. It means no longer waiting at home for the love of your life to find you, but taking action to go and find love. With a mindset like this, you make your life begin rather than waiting for it to start around you.

Gaining the initiative in your own life will empower you and allow you to take control of what happens in your life. You become more active and decisive in daily life and you will find yourself ready to take on any challenges that come your way.

PRINCIPLE 2

CHANGE IS NOT YOUR ENEMY

Many people fear the unfamiliar, fear change, and in this fast-paced postmodern world, constant change has become a big source of stress. People nowadays change jobs and change relationship partners fairly quickly, and the lack of security and familiarity can take it's toll. There are many people who struggle and resist so hard, trying to prevent change from happening, but the truth is, no one can ever really stop change.

Many schools of thought, from the east to the west, uphold the premise that the only constant in life is change, and humans must adapt and act accordingly in order to survive. Unwillingness to accept change will only serve to alienate and frustrate you. But why are there some people who are so afraid of change?

The need for control

It can be pretty scary when something in life changes, especially if it's something that you did not anticipate. You can feel like you're losing control of your life, you can even feel small and insignificant, which, for those who have always exercised or valued control, can be devastating. But you have to remember that the only thing you can truly control is how you respond to abrupt or even unwelcome changes that come into your life. You have to accept that you can't control everything; all you can do is be prepared and try to make the best decisions that you can when change does come your way.

See change as a challenge and an opportunity

When you find that things are changing, that figurative doors are opening and closing before you, you can get confused and doubtful, after all, there is great comfort in familiarity and routine. But there is another way to view change that can be more helpful and productive for you, view change as a challenge that you can conquer and an opportunity to reach greater heights. This way, you will be able to accept change more readily, as well as adapt yourself to the changes that are happening around you.

Being Active

Knowing that change is inevitable and being prepared for these changes will allow you to actively take part in the change. Rather than being paralyzed with fear at what might happen or stubbornly rejecting the change already happening around you, you can be present in the situation. Through this view of change, you can take part and be an active component, and ultimately, you can gain leverage over the situation more effectively by taking appropriate actions.

By accepting that change constantly in life, you will be able to go with the ebb and flow with more stability than those who refuse to acknowledge change. Realize that change brings about new opportunities as well as challenges that can only help you to grow and become a better person. After all, to be successful, you need to be prepared and willing to get out of your comfort zone and step into the fray. In short, you must be someone who is not afraid to face change head on.

PRINCIPLE 3

WHY YOU ARE WHAT YOU THINK

How you perceive yourself is an important part of how you actually turn out to be. From the moment you open your eyes, your mind runs on with how you perceive the world. These thoughts hold powerful sway over you, but most people do not really think much about that. How you think is something so simple and fundamental that many people just take it for granted. But how you see the world affects how the world actually is in relation to you, and it affects how your life turns out to be. Thoughts can be the only thing standing between you and a happy and contented life.

Once you realize the power of thoughts, you will be able to make use of such thoughts to turn your life around. Making use of the power of the mind to bring about positive change is an easier way of finding true happiness.

Get in touch with the quiet

Every day, you are faced with a barrage of ideas, opinions, negative feedback, and whatnot, and you have to find a way to get back to the peace and quiet inside of you. By getting in touch with yourself again, you can find your inner self and realize true contentment with yourself. Your inner self is pure and separate from all the negativity around you, which is why you need to concentrate and shut off all these negative thoughts. Turn off your cellphone, computer, TV, etc., and sit quietly. Try to rid your mind of the usual clutter and concentrate on the calm. Develop a sense of well-being in this calm. You can even just go for a walk, at the same time being aware of all the things around you.

Remind yourself

Keep notes of what you want to remember. The human mind is wired to remember negative things more than positive things. It is part of survival, as evolution has literally made failure traumatic for you so that you won't repeat it. Failure, in your pre-historic past, could have meant death. But this is no longer the case. You know that failure and mistakes are part of the human experience. Everyone makes mistakes and these actually make you a better person. You can change this wiring of your brain. You can choose to remember the positive, not forgetting to take lessons from the mistakes though. You can choose to do some meditation or repeat affirmations to yourself. You can leave little encouraging notes for yourself wherever possible. Remember that you are a wonderful person and that you live a great life full of joy.

What you think and how you see yourself greatly affects your life. It is important that you be mindful of your own thoughts. Don't let negativity gain ground and run away with you. Remind yourself of the good things in your life, of your accomplishments, of the simple things in your life that make you smile. Think positive thoughts so that you can live a positive life.

PRINCIPLE 4

KEEP YOUR MIND OPEN TO NEW IDEAS

In order to continue learning and growing as a person and as a professional, you have to stay open to new ideas. After all, no matter how much you've already learned, there will always be new advancements in science, sales, education etc. that you can still continue to learn and make use of. Also, everyone has acquired different points of view and versions of knowledge, all of which hold their own particular truths. If you end up only acknowledging your own personal truth and knowledge, you become out of touch and alienated.

Let go of preconceptions and never assume anything

Thinking that you already know all there is to be known about a certain subject can make you blind to many new and revolutionary ideas. Being open to new ideas means letting go of whatever preconception you may have in any given field. Try to look at everything with fresh eyes. There are times when, after being trained to see something as bad, you totally ignore or miss all the possible benefits from it. This is especially true when listening or deliberating new techniques or strategies at work. Standing by preconceptions based on flimsy information can make you blind to many new and exciting possibilities around you.

Assumption without proper investigation or information can prove to be a huge thorn on your side. Important decisions have to be based upon solid information and studies in order to be effective. Assuming anything unfounded as the truth can lead you to making bad decisions, and assuming that you already know everything you need to know can leave you falling flat and left behind. Make sure that whatever you hold as true is based on solid facts and figures so you don't end up making misinformed decisions that could have negative repercussions.

Work with a clear vision

Preconceptions and biases are like dark clouds that keep you from seeing things for how they actually are. They blur your vision and keep you from seeing the actual reality around you. But in order for you to make the best decision possible, you will need to have a clear vision of where you stand and where you are headed. This way, you can accurately weigh your options and choose the best course of action.

Hear others out

Always keep in mind that new perspectives and points of view offer fresh input, it doesn't matter who they come from. Even the person talking is a fresh graduate or a seasoned veteran, it is always a good idea to hear them out, and it may prove to be worth your while. Everyone has their own take on something, and combining these different views may allow you to reach the best solution or take on the matter.

Being open to new ideas means that you continue to grow and learn. You are not content with the knowledge you have already acquired and instead, you continue to seek out more to stay on top of the game and be the best in your profession.

PRINCIPLE 5

LIFE IS HOW YOU EXPERIENCE IT

Everyone goes through ups and downs. Everyone, no matter how rich or powerful, has, at some point, experienced failure. There is no one in the world who can claim that he or she has succeeded in every single venture he has embarked upon, and there is no one in history who can claim that they have never been disappointed. But how everyone reacts to the difficulties life throws at them greatly differs from person to person, and therein lies the key.

Life is full of suffering

In life you feel pain, sadness, fear, anger and doubt. In the same sense, you also feel joy, love, kinship, and fulfillment. Everyone has a reason to feel all these emotions, everyone has a reason to be sad, or happy, to feel loved or feel fear. No matter who you are, life is life, and the big difference is how one chooses to experience it. Of course, anyone can say that it is easy to be happy if you are rich, with the perfect house, the dream car, and the perfect job, but there are plenty of rich and famous people who are unhappy. On the other hand, there are people living in poverty who still find simple pleasures and happiness, living out their days knowing more joy than the most affluent. This only means that happiness is not all about possessions.

You have a choice

How your life is can be equated to how you perceive and experience it. If you view and experience your life through negativity, dissatisfaction, and pessimism, then it will be a negative, dark, and unhappy life. But if you choose to view and live life through eyes filled with love, appreciation, and optimism, then your life becomes happy and cherished. Always remember that even though you can't change the circumstances you were born in or how your life has turned out, you can always change the quality in which you experience and respond to life. Always remember that you have a choice. You can choose to agonize over every regrettable mistake, or worry over the uncertainty of the future, or you can choose to accept and forgive yourself for your mistakes and look into the future with hope and positivity. You can choose to be frustrated and dissatisfied, or you can choose to be happy and content.

Taking the road to change

Changing the way you think and experience life so you can have a more positive outlook is a long road with bumps along the way. Changing your outlook and how you see the world will take time and patience, but simply making that choice is already a big step towards the mastery over your own life. Decide to live your life to the fullest, cherish every moment of it, get on track towards positive change, and reach success with satisfaction. Once you realize that how you experience life is under your control, you can finally start taking control of your life and experience it in the purest, most positive light.

PRINCIPLE 6

WHY IT'S NEVER TOO LATE TO START FRESH

Once you reach a certain age, there are already things that are expected of you that you might or might not have achieved. You might even find yourself in a place you didn't want to be in, or, when you reached the top of your mountain of dreams, you realize that it was not what you had expected or wanted. Feeling like you are trapped in a position or job that you don't like, much less love, is something too many people feel. It can be frustrating and draining to continue working and doing something you don't care about. But here's news for you, you can ALWAYS start fresh, no matter how old you are or how long you've been doing it.

Your personal satisfaction is important, too

A lot of people end up feeling like they're stuck simply because their financial status dictates that they keep this job that is slowly sucking their lives away, but this is never true. You are never really trapped. You always have options and you can always choose to turn your career into one that caters to your needs, rather than just the other way around. The aspect that is important here is that you find out what you truly want in life, find out what will give your life direction and meaning, and once you have a clear idea of where you want to be and what you want to do, you can start working on how you will get there.

Don't be afraid to start something new

You have to have confidence in yourself and your capabilities. Do not be afraid to go out there and start again. Remember that you are not starting from scratch, you still have the abilities and experience that you had worked to achieve, which you can use to your advantage as you start on this new chapter of your life. Have confidence in yourself and your capabilities, and don't be afraid to take that chance. Letting an opportunity go by might turn into the biggest regret of your life.

Have a plan and take it one step at a time

It can be difficult, however, to choose to start fresh when you already have a family to support. It can be a different matter entirely once you have your children and spouse's financial security on the line. If this is the case, and if you find yourself at a loss on how to start, you can always start by devising a plan. Quitting your job right away may not be the smartest move for you at this point, but you can always take baby steps in the beginning. Start by doing something during your free time, something that you really like to do, and then form a plan that can make the transition easier for you and your family's financial security. Make sure the plan is solid and realistic or else, you'll be setting yourself up for failure and disappointment.

Do not be afraid to make a move once you feel that you are becoming stagnant in your job. Don't be afraid to take the chance to finally enjoy your life.

PRINCIPLE 7

THE CAPACITY FOR ACCEPTANCE

Having the capacity to accept every single part of oneself is something that can be difficult for many, which is why there are so many people who drown the truth about themselves in lies and half-truths. Rather than accepting their weaknesses and actively working in order to improve themselves, they would rather turn a blind eye, which only serves to make the said problems worse. On the other hand, seeing only weaknesses, while unable to recognize strengths, can make one lose confidence and doubt oneself. A balance in self-perception must be found because every day, people are flooded with images of what should be the ideal and what they should be striving for, with no thought left for how things actually are.

With the constant bombardment of this type of advertising, people end up trying to emulate an ideal concept of what someone should be and what someone should own without even being aware of who they really are and unwilling to accept the harsh truths. How can anyone become the best version of themselves if they cannot even honestly see who they are in the present?

Just Acceptance

In order to attain your goals of self-improvement, you have to accept yourself and your circumstances first. Acceptance, in this sense, refers to being aware of every aspect of your being without any judgment and biases. This means being able to see all sides of yourself in neutrality, or, in the purest sense of the word. It is an awareness that is open and encompassing. Without acceptance, as it is with change, you can become frustrated and bitter about life, but being able to accept yourself, taking the positive along with the negative, and being able to accept the difficulties of life means you are prepping yourself to start moving on.

Rid the mind of judgmental thoughts

Acceptance must be done without judgment, or else it is not acceptance at all. You have to rid yourself of preconceptions and biases before you can learn to accept anything. Being judgmental of yourself, your way of life, and your circumstances can only lead to more suffering as you agonize over the unfairness, trials, and difficulties you have to face. There is nothing that can justify this kind of mental self-harm, for as you pity yourself and rage over the injustices, you are also stuck, wallowing in the negativity. See the good and the bad in yourself just as they are, and keep yourself from blame and guilt when it comes to your shortcomings. Simply be aware, and then finally, accept.

An active approach after acceptance

Once you learn to accept yourself for who you are, you will then be able to take on an active role in your life. The minute you rid yourself of judgment, you can then focus your mind into making positive and purposeful actions that can lead to betterment; you are finally free to take actions. With acceptance, you can finally move on in life and strive for success.

PRINCIPLE 8

FINDING YOUR TRUE HAPPINESS

Everyone has their own concept of happiness, but not all of these are equal to true happiness. Sure, watching a movie can make you laugh, and buying something new can satisfy you, but these pleasures are hardly ever long term. Before you know it, you have to go out and find the next distraction, the next big purchase that will make you "happy." This is not true happiness. True happiness is a feeling that cannot be bought and is always present, even after the movie has ended or the new things get old. True happiness is found inside you, not in external or material things.

Find Your True Self

Before you can achieve true happiness, you have to stop looking at the pretty things or trying to project a certain image into the world, and start looking in. Only through reflection of self can you see the real you and discover the happiness and peace that already resides inside of you. You have to do away with all the passing thoughts, worries, and regrets that swirl around your true self, and once you clear all that away, you will find the wisdom inside of you. You have to learn to see and content with who you are. Only by doing this can you truly realize that you don't need material things or other people's admiration to be happy and content.

Develop a positive nature

You will always have a choice on how you want to see and experience the world. You are never helpless, and you are never forced to retain a negative view of the world. You can always CHOOSE to be more positive. You can choose to see the brightness of the day and enjoy the simple things. Like the proverbial story about the two prisoners in the tiny cell with only a small window, you can choose to see the sky rather than the dirt. It is only your mind that limits you.

Your negative experiences do not define you

People who have lost an arm or a leg have the tendency to see themselves as only that, someone missing a limb. Added to this is the all too common feelings of pity and awkwardness that people feel for someone who has lost a limb, and this is understandable. But this negative aspect does not define you or anyone else. There are men and women everywhere who still excel at sports, business, and academics who have lost their limbs, some even more than one, or have lost control of their body. Being a paraplegic or amputee does not define them; it is their will, their desire to excel, and their heart that makes the difference. These may be extreme examples but the truth stands, negative experiences do not define you, and dwelling on them will not allow you to get any closer to realizing true happiness. You are not your problems.

Finding true happiness is when your true self has been revealed to you and you loved it. There is pure, wholesome, unchanging contentment, and happiness within you that do not need material compensation. It is happiness that is free.

PRINCIPLE 9

THE IMPACT OF POSITIVE THINKING

It often happens that you cannot control how things happen around you, but you can control your attitude towards them. Having a positive attitude is an important part of living a full-life, and not only that, it also has big effects on the way you think, how you learn, and the quality of your life.

Positive thoughts broaden your perspective

Negative thoughts and emotions have a very specific effect on how you think. When faced with a negative situation, which your brain perceives as a threat to your life and well-being, for example, when you feel fear or anger, there are only two concepts that are primarily retained, fight or flight. This way of reacting to negative or threatening situations stem from man's primitive roots, when getting out of danger and having a one track mind on how to go about it was the most important thing for survival. But in modern times, this evolutionary trait has become a hindrance. It often happens that these threatening situations are not life and death, i.e. instead of a wolf in the forest, it just happens to be a rather stressful day at work. Negative thoughts limit your mind's capacity to think. When you focus on the negative, your mind tends to limit the options you see around you, just as it would if you had been faced with a hungry wolf, you either flee or fight. On the other hand, positive thoughts tend to broaden your perspective, giving you the capacity to imagine many possibilities and outcomes. Research has shown that people who are prone to positive thoughts recognize more possibilities and opportunities compared to people exposed to negative thoughts and emotions.

Positivity helps you Learn

Because thinking positive thoughts broaden your perceptions and mindset, it also helps you develop more skills. A happy person who is not afraid to go out there and try new things will be able to learn and retain more of what he or she has learned rather than someone who is closed off to the same possibilities. With positive thinking, you can develop new interests and skillsets that can become important resources for you in the future. On the other hand, negative emotions will actually limit your development as it keeps your mind from imagining all these new and exciting possibilities, and keeps you too preoccupied in negativity to do anything fun or out of the ordinary.

Develop Positive Thinking

There are many ways you can develop positive thinking. Research has shown that meditation, or at least having some guided quiet time, increases the sense of wellness and connectedness that easily converts to happiness. Taking time to do things that are fun and enjoyable for you with people you love is also a great way to stay positive. Find something that works for you and consciously try to develop more positive thoughts and views.

Being happy is not only the result of success, it is a precursor to it as well. Maintaining a positive mindset helps you achieve success much more easily than being a grump, and it makes the journey towards success a lot more fun, too!

"GETTING FREE OF OUR OBSTACLES, IS THE SUREST WAY TO FIND OUR TRUE GREATNESS AND ACHIEVE THE MOST SUCCESS."

> "Mistakes are just stepping stones to the top of the mountain."

PRINCIPLE 10

YOU MUST NOT BE AFRAID TO MAKE MISTAKES

The thought of making mistakes can be scary to a lot of people because of the negative implications and emotions associated with it. Making a mistake can seem like it reflects on your knowledge, experience and expertise (when it comes to making a mistake in your profession), making you feel vulnerable, less confident, and less competent than you might have been.

No one in the world welcomes the idea of making mistakes, but the truth is that it is inevitable. Everyone, no matter how brilliant, smart or wealthy, makes mistakes. Always being sure of everything means that you view the world as unchanging, but it never is. There is nothing fixed in the world and as you venture forth, you are bound to stumble. Although it may seem like a horrible situation to make mistakes, in the end, there is still a gain from them.

You can learn from them

When you make mistakes, it can feel horrible, almost crippling, but you have to learn to get past that initial negative feeling and turn it into action. Once you realize that you've made a mistake, you can then learn how not to do it in the future, or at least how to do it better. Making mistakes can be the best teacher there is. You will learn your lessons quickly and there is little chance that you would forget them. Facts and knowledge that once seemed inconceivable to you can become clear, and you will end up having to face your shortcomings directly rather than skirting past them as you may have in the past.

Mistakes can get you back to earth

Sometimes, you lose touch of who you are as you ride on a high of success and triumph, but making mistakes can get you back to earth and show you the gritty reality. Flying too close to the sun can burn you, but errors will help to ground you and make you stay humble. Know that no one is perfect, that no one is infallible and that no matter how hard you try, mistakes will happen. The best you can do is learn to pick yourself up, dust yourself off, and do better.

Seeing mistakes as opportunities and challenges

You can change the way your mind perceives the world in order to see mistakes in a different and more positive light. See the world as ever changing, that nothing is fixed or absolute and you will be more forgiving of your mistakes. You know that there is always something that is different from the last time you saw it and you realize that there is so much to learn. You know that the mistakes you make will only improve on your overall understanding of something.

Once you realize that mistakes are inevitable in the ever-changing process of life, you will no longer come to fear it. Mistakes are natural and the best that you can do is own up to them and learn from them.

PRINCIPLE 11

FINDING GOOD MOTIVATIONS

Getting up every day can be a struggle for anyone if they don't have motivation. Being motivated is what makes people strive for excellence and do their work with passion. It is what makes people wake up early and work hard every day. Without motivation, there is no reason to do anything, no thirst for life and what life has to offer, which is why it is important to find good motivations that will help you reach your full potential.

Most people have their motivations but often for different reasons. Motivations can be divided into two types: there is intrinsic, something within, and extrinsic, something from outside, motivation. Intrinsic motivation is the basic human desire to explore boundaries, to reach peaks and go beyond, to rise to the occasion and be challenged.

Extrinsic motivation, on the other hand, is the type of motivation that promises reward. A promotion, a new car, a fat check, these are all extrinsic motivations. This means that you do a task not because you want to, but for the promise of something else or to keep yourself from negative consequences. This means getting up in the morning to work a job you dislike because you have to pay the bills, or doing something you personally don't believe in as you might end up getting demoted otherwise, or lose the promotion you're eyeing. You are doing something because you have to, not because you want to.

Getting motivation from what you do, not what you get

The desire to become an expert in something, the desire to be helpful, the desire to work hard for a worthy cause, the desire to become a better person, these are all intrinsic motivations. These are motivations that come with passion, conviction, and drive. You do your task because you believe in it, because you know that you will become a better person, because it is something that is worthwhile to you, and most importantly, because you want to do what you do. Expanding your capabilities and living up to your full potential is a very natural human need, and being motivated to do the right thing simply because it is the right thing is a noble attribute and gives your life quality and vibrancy.

Weighing motivations

Having to do something simply because you have to (i.e. financial reasons, fear of blame or guilt) affects how you do the task itself. Surely you have noticed that when you put your heart and soul into something, the result is drastically different than when you are doing something you resent simply because you have no other choice.

Motivations affect the quality of your work, as well as the quality of your life. The more you steer yourself towards intrinsic motivations, where you do things because you find them fulfilling and you are passionate about it, the happier you are and the fuller your life becomes. Success is easier to achieve when you do your work with conviction and drive, and your occupation is also your passion.

PRINCIPLE 12

WHY YOU SHOULD DREAM BIG

Dreaming big can seem like a corny cliché, but the truth is, dreams fuel how you live your life. Big dreamers tend to be more passionate, more driven, and even more successful simply because they did not give up and were willing to go the extra mile for their dreams. Big dreamers are also willing to get disappointed and fail now and then, because they have dreams that fuel them. If you want to have a meaningful life that you can be proud of, you have to start by following your dreams. And if you're going to dream, why not dream big? Why not aim for the stars? There's still a chance you can reach for it, after all.

Dreams inspire you

Having dreams, no matter how lofty or seemingly impossible they can be, give you direction and inspiration. Your dreams give you reason to work hard and have hope for a better future. Keeping the dream alive inside of you fuels your drive to keep going despite setback and hardships. Your dreams can connect you to your true self, and following your dreams will bring you happiness that cannot be equaled by any amount of wealth or comfort. The dream inside you is what can keep you going because you are fueled by a passion that burns for itself and not any other material reward.

Big dreams give meaning and purpose to your life

Big dreams can change a person's life for the better. These dreams that you have can spur you on to keep trying even when people or even logic tells you otherwise. These dreams give you purpose. Because you choose to dream big, you can live a meaningful life that enriches your soul and can even enrich the world. The people who have changed the world were those who were willing to dream big dreams that everyone thought were crazy, from Galileo to Van Gogh to Martin Luther King, all these people chose to follow their dreams despite adversity, and by doing so, they have affected positive change into the world.

Because there is hope you'll achieve them

When you hold true to your dreams, you are also keeping hope alive in your heart. If you continue to hope and strive for your dreams, there will always be that chance that you can reach it, and even if you don't, you will have spent your life with the joy of knowing that you lived the best way any one can, never idle, with a dream in your thoughts and hope in your heart.

It is a sad thing indeed when a child's dreams are washed away by cold reality. Sometimes, there are people at the end of their lives who end up wondering where their dreams went, for as they look back in their lives, they find it missing a quality, a spark. You can choose to keep this spark going until the very end; you can choose to keep dreaming.

PRINCIPLE 13

FOLLOW YOUR PASSIONS

There is a big difference between a job that you have to do, and a job that you love to do, and surely, you are able to see that there is a big difference in the outcomes. Being passionate about something and working hard to uphold or achieve it is one of the things that give life meaning and purpose. Finding and following your passions will strengthen your commitment and motivation, and increases the fulfillment that you feel in life, as opposed to the things that you do simply because you need to pay the bills.

You have to give yourself time to find out what you are really passionate about, and try to fit it into your life. Your passion might be for something that is not profitable or viable as a fulltime occupation, but you can try to do it during your free time. No matter what it is, if you are passionate about it, then it is worth pursuing. Remember that life is only lived once, and that regrets are always too late. You can't always just be practical, you need your noble cause, your dragon to vanquish, you damsel to save, in order for you to say that you have, in the truest sense of the word, lived.

Success is sweeter with passion

Success is something that everyone strives for, but successes can also have varied values. Being successful in something that you don't really care for is not as satisfying as being successful in something you worked hard on and believed in. Being passionate about your craft or profession drives you to succeed, and this passion will also make your quest for achievement and betterment unshakable. This is because you do it for the sake of doing it, because you believe that what you do HAS to be done and done well, this in itself will make your work seem less like a job. If you truly love what you do, then it will seem as if you never have to work a day in your life.

Your passion for your work will give life more meaning

Going to work every day full of drive and enthusiasm means a better quality of life and brings you much closer to achieving success in what you do. Being passionate about what you do will make your life more meaningful and fulfilling. It brings about a sense of well-being, a sense of satisfaction in your life that cannot be brought about by buying expensive things or living in luxury. What good is luxury anyway if you hate your job, or you have no meaning in your life?

Pursuing your passions will allow you to grow as a person, as a worker, as an artist etc. and allow you to achieve your true potential. It is only through pursuing your passions that you open the doors toward true self-empowerment. By following your passions, your sense of self-worth grows exponentially with every day that you continue the work that you love to do and believe in it wholeheartedly.

PRINCIPLE 14

THINKING OUTSIDE THE BOX

Thinking outside the box is an expression that means not letting your mind and ideas get boxed in or limited by preconceived notions or how things are and should be. Thinking outside the box means you are able to exercise your creativity, innovativeness, and originality. When it comes to problem solving or starting out in a new aspect of your life, whether personal or professional, thinking outside the box will give you more solutions and answers that you might not have thought of before.

But how is it done? How do you make sure you're not letting yourself get boxed in when it comes to thinking up solutions to certain problems?

When you approach a problem already knowing, or at least you think so, what the best solution would be, you are already boxing yourself in. Don't be content with the easy formulas that you already know. Thinking outside the box means approaching a problem in a wholly different view. But how can you see a problem through different lenses? By learning a new approach.

Study outside of your profession and let your creativity flow

This doesn't mean you have to go to school again, although this can be an option if you have the time and finances for it; you can simply opt to read up on a topic that is separate from your profession or industry but is nevertheless interesting to you. Read up on education and leadership, or sales and marketing, or whatever topic interests you in other industries or professions.

You might discover that there are problems that are related to or similar to the ones you are facing, but with a wholly different approach when solving such problems.

Take some time out and get into one of your hobbies. Draw, write, paint - all these activities activate the right hemisphere of the brain that is responsible for creativity. You can even write some rhyming poetry to get your mind to open up to new rhythms and solutions. Zone out for a little bit and do some of these creative activities, and you might find yourself suddenly yelling out "Eureka!"

Turn it inside out, upside down, or go backwards

Approaching a problem from a different angle or going at it from another way can help you see it in a new and separate light, which can then offer up solutions and insight that may not have been evident before. You can do this metaphorically, by visualizing it, or literally, by flipping a piece of paper, model, or blueprint, etc. to help you see the problem from another angle. Working backwards is the same, but this time, you visualize or start your planning on where you want to be then go backwards until you reach your current situation. This way, you can take a step back from your mind's usual hardwiring.

Thinking outside the box may seem like a cliché, but it is actually a way to get your mind away from overused solutions. It is about taking on problems using new and creative ideas that are wholly your own.

PRINCIPLE 15

PERSONAL GROWTH

No matter where you are in life, there will always be room for growth, whether it's intellectual, emotional, or spiritual, which means that through life, you can continue to strive to be better. Even if you were an expert at something, even if you have a PhD, or you believe you've achieved the things you always wanted, there will always be room to grow. Personal growth is what drives human beings to become better, to change, to improve, to be the best that they can be and make the world a bit better in their little way.

Improve yourself for yourself

The desire for personal growth should not be about outdoing anyone else, or to be recognized and applauded, it should simply be about you and how you want to grow as a person. It can be about becoming more confident, or being patient or learning to let go of regrets and grudges, it can be about whatever part of your personality that you want to improve. It can even be about your physical health, such as wanting to eat healthier and exercising more often so that you can enjoy your life more. Anything in your life that you want to make better means there's room and opportunity for you to grow. Wanting to improve yourself however, does not mean that you are not happy with who you are, it simply means the desire to become the best that you can be. Do not denigrate yourself and your abilities, you're already great, but surely you can be better.

Learn from the past

A good way of achieving personal growth is by learning from the past. There are people in this world who end up making the same mistakes over and over, whether it is in relationships, in their profession, or their personal life. They can get angry and frustrated when the same things keep happening again and again, but they never really try to root why these things happen. But to get out of the loop, one has to root out the problem.

Rooting out the problem

When going through something like this, you can ask yourself questions like, *"Why did I let him/her treat me this way?"* Or *"Why did I lash out on my family?"* Or *"Why do I have a bad relationship with my co-workers?"* Once you get to the meat of the matter, you can flesh out the reasons behind the problems and work on those. If you find that you have low self-esteem, or a short temper then you can work on those by being conscious of that weakness and striving to improve yourself in that aspect. This can be done by simply being present and mindful of how you act, or by putting on some extra effort when it comes to that particular aspect.

Personal growth is an important part of becoming a successful, positive, and dynamic person. It is only through the constant desire to be better that you actually become your best.

PRINCIPLE 16

BECOME MINDFUL

Being mindful is a state of being ever aware, ever present, and living in the moment. Life, after all, is just a series of moments strung together, and it is up to the individual whether to cherish these moments or let them be forgettable.

As it often happens nowadays, people's minds are so preoccupied with worrying over the future or regretting mistakes or decisions made in the past that they forget to live in the moment. But what does living in the moment mean and how do you stay in the moment?

Be present, wherever you are, all the time

Have you ever heard the phrase "physically present but mentally absent"? This pertains to when a person is physically in a certain place but they have their minds drifting away. Being somewhere else in your head is a normal reaction if you happen to always be stressed or if you have important things that you have to take care of or find a solution for, but this also makes you miss out on a lot of life's simple but substantial joys. Being preoccupied with negative thoughts and fantasies cloud your perception and appreciation of the world around you, and makes you oblivious to whatever little miracles are actually already happening around you. It's these little moments that make life worth living, but with your mind somewhere else, how can you even be aware of them?

Do your best to be mentally present wherever you are and

whatever it is you are doing. Empty your mind of worries and regrets and live the present moment to the fullest, after all, the present is all that you really have. Whenever you find your thoughts wandering toward the future or agonizing over the past, gently direct your awareness back to the present moment, whether you're at dinner with your family or simply taking a walk through the park on your own.

Being mindful means being at peace

With mindfulness, you can learn to become more at peace with yourself and your life. If you allow your thoughts to run away with you all the time, it means that your mind is not resolved to where your physical body is at present. Your mind wants to run away, go back, or fast forward to a time that is better. But being aware of your present is learning to be at peace with where you are and who you are. With mindfulness, you can learn to appreciate your life as it is now, and you can learn to live day to day. You can learn to live as life happens around you.

Mindfulness is a very helpful state of mind when it comes to becoming calm and letting go of stressful thoughts. It allows you to be free of negativity and leaves room in your mind to appreciate and be involved in all the things that are happening around you. Mindfulness brings about peace of mind, positivity, and sensitivity to all things around you, making your life fuller and more significant.

PRINCIPLE 17

BEFORE YOU START SOMETHING...

There comes a time in everyone's life that they're struck by a great idea. But no matter how great the idea might be, there are a few considerations you have to take into account. Having a great idea is different from having a marketable or practical plan.

Without planning, a lot of great ideas can't get off the ground, and a lot of those that do take off tend to crash and burn in the first few years. You have to follow up your great idea to make sure that it becomes a viable investment. What are the factors that you have to consider for your start-up idea?

- It has to be needed and useful. You have to make sure that your product actually fills in a need that people have. Sure, you can add colors and glitter, even have a catchy name for your product, but the bottomline is still whether the service or product you are offering has quality that will get customers to buy it. If you truly want to create or start something that will last, make sure that it is useful in a certain way. Whether it's a general need that everyone can find use for or you're targeting a specific market, your product has to be able to find a niche and fill a need.

- It has to be different and original. Once you've established that your idea is something that people actually need, you have to take a look around. Are there products, concepts, or services already offer the same thing as you are offering? If not, then great, you have an original idea. But if you recognize the same concept in other products or companies, then you have to ask yourself: What makes my idea different, or even better, than what's already out in the market? This is the time that you have to innovate. If there still isn't anything that makes your product different from others, then you have to think of a way to make your product standout. And if you can't do that, then maybe you should consider entering another market.

- Continued improvements. A good turnout in the beginning doesn't mean a good turnout forever. Constant improvement and innovation are important if you want to keep going and stay in the business for the long run. People are always looking for something new and improved, and your ability to innovate can be the difference between survival and the end of your great idea.

- Financially viable. You need to have a clear view of where you want to go and where you are starting out in the beginning. How much money do you have to spend on launching your project and what kind of returns are you expecting? When do you expect these returns? Knowing the financial projections can save you a lot of worry and will dictate how you launch your project. With proper planning, this little side-project can even turn into a livelihood.

Your ideas might just be a goldmine, but only if you plan it out carefully and continuously. A good idea has to be followed up well for it to actually become viable in the end.

"OUR LIVES ARE LARGELY THE RESULT OF THE ACTIONS THAT WE TAKE EACH DAY. ARE YOU TAKING ACTIONS THAT MOVE YOU FORWARD TO THE FUTURE YOU DESIRE OR ARE YOU ENGAGED IN TIME-WASTING, WORTHLESS ACTIVITY?"

PRINCIPLE 18

CLEAR AWAY THE STRESS

Stress is ever present in today's society. It is with you in the car as you sit in traffic, it is looking over your shoulder as you take a look at the current month's bills, it is in bed next to you as you worry over the events of the day. Letting stress take free reign of your mind can lead to many serious health and mental issues, which is why it is important that you manage stress and find a way to relax and still be positive despite the stressors that can come pouring in.

Identify the root of the stress

In order to manage stress more efficiently, you have to be able to pinpoint where it stems from. You have to identify whether the stress you are constantly under is due to internal or external factors. You might be stressed out because you tend to fall behind at work, or the deadlines keep creeping up on you, but it might be the fact that you tend to put things off until the last minute which causes the stress rather than the actual work that you have to do. Are you stressed out at work because of the attitude of your co-workers or boss, or are you just the type of person who tends to overthink and agonize over everything? Knowing the basis for your stress is important if you want to manage it effectively.

Control the internal factors

Once you identify the internal source of your stress, i.e. your tendency to procrastinate or your need for control, then you can start to take steps to change your mindset and your usual pattern when faced with stress. You can try to develop a timetable so that you can manage your time better, or start teaching yourself to let go and compromise in situations that are out of your control. Unless you alter the behavior and way of thinking that causes the stress, then you will never be able to manage it.

Avoid the external factors

When your stressor is external to you and out of your control, the best way to manage is by avoiding it. If certain social interactions stress you out, then avoid them. For example, if going to parties with loud music and dancing causes stress to you, don't go. Limit your social interactions to those that are comfortable and relaxing for you, such as having coffee with an old friend, or having a lovely dinner. It is the same when it comes to a person who stresses you out. If you find a certain person stressful to be around, then limit the time you spend with them.

Also, avoid getting into situations that you know can be overwhelming for you and would just stress you out. Learn to say no when you think you already have a lot on your plate or if you know the situation will only cause you stress. Knowing your limits and not letting yourself get overwhelmed with work and responsibilities is a great way to manage stress.

PRINCIPLE 19

FORM CLEAR CUT GOALS

Forming clear cut goals is important if you want to achieve success. Knowing where you are headed and when you intend to get there adds to your motivation and drive to work hard for your goals. Having a clear set of goals is important for your focus and enthusiasm in doing your work, as you have a clear vision on what you want to achieve as you toil away.

Set solid short-term goals that lead up to your long-term goal

Having clear cut goals will help you set achievable short term goals that can add fuel to the flames of your perseverance. Achieving minor, short term goals will help your self-esteem and confidence in making minor decisions as you continue to hone your craft and set your sight towards your end goal. These short-term goals help to keep you from burning out, providing you with little triumphs that can give a great deal of satisfaction.

On the other hand, having a clear view of your long term goals will give you a clear view of why you are sacrificing and working hard, making it all worth it in the end. Having a clear view of your long-term goal will also make decision making easier for you as you have a clear view of what you want to achieve.

Forming clear cut goals can make it easier to achieve them

With a clear view of what you want to achieve, you can optimize your time and resources to make it fit into your timeline for what you want to achieve. You can also plan your course of actions as you set out to achieve them and not waste any of the limited resources you have on things that end up being ineffectual in the big picture. You will also be able to measure your progress more effectively, as well as the efficiency of your strategies in attaining your goals.

Your efforts will also be more focused once you have clear cut goals, as having a clear vision of what you want to achieve will allow you to direct your thoughts into how you can achieve them. This will foster creativity and out-of-the-box thinking that can lead to more innovations in your business or field.

Clear cut goals make you stand out

With clear cut goals, you will be able to effectively communicate whatever you want to achieve to your clients and or co-workers. This means that they will have a clear idea of what you have to offer and what you want to attain, and they will also have a clear grasp of what they will get (as a customer) and what they can contribute (as an employee or co-worker). This clear communication and branding can help in sales (if that's where you are) as well as efficiency within the workplace.

Setting clear cut goals will give a clear idea on how, when, what you are going to achieve them with. This makes it easier for you to measure progress and make swift decisions that can greatly benefit you and get you closer to success.

PRINCIPLE 20

USING STRATEGIC PLANNING TO ACHIEVE SUCCESS

The more thought out and well-planned something is, the better its execution. This is the same with life. The better you plan out your short-term and long-term goals, the better your chances are to achieve them and the closer you get to success. This is where strategic planning comes in. With strategic planning, you can reach your goals in the fastest way possible with the least difficulty, rather than just winging it, so to speak.

Strategic planning or goal setting is a skill that anyone can learn. If you start out with a bit of difficulty, don't worry, because it will get easier with time and it is something that you can apply into your daily life as well as professional and business goals.

Strategic planning aims to find the most practical and profitable way to run your business

With strategic planning, you will be able to restructure your company or business so that it maximizes all resources and employees efficiently. You will be able to get more work done and with better quality if you plan out how everything works. This way you can fix any areas that may be facing problems and improve certain areas that show weakness. If you use strategic planning effectively, you will soon see the results through an increase in profit, enhanced efficiency and higher yield when it comes to investments.

Strategic planning in everyday life

Applying strategic planning in your daily life has the same concept as in business, but instead of profit and efficiency, you want to earn more vitality and happiness. In this sense, you are investing your mental and physical capacities on different aspects of your life. With strategic planning, you can try to find the best ways to use your energies that promise the highest yield when it comes to more energy, vitality, and joy. This way, you won't be wasting time and energy on things that only end up giving you headaches anyway.

Strategic planning means being open to revision and fine-tuning

Strategic planning is never fixed. You can change it and fine-tune whenever you feel the need. Never allow your misconceptions limit you. You have to realize that the world, along with business, constantly changes. The market you planned for may experience a big shift that you did not anticipate, or the person that you've been spending so much of your time and energy on may have a change of heart. Sticking to an outmoded plan can be the kiss of death. Know that just because you have to change your strategy doesn't mean you have failed. The time when you don't adapt to the changes happening around you is when you will fail. Once you find that your plans are zapping energy and profit from you, take the time to analyze the situation again and apply changes to address the issue.

Using strategic planning can help you achieve the best that you can without exhausting yourself or wasting too much of your own resources.

PRINCIPLE 21

DEVELOP A STRONG WORK ETHIC

A strong work ethic is something you will need if you want to get far. This set of principles will be your guiding light as you trudge up the mountain of effort to reach your dreams, and these principles will also be the equipment that you can use in order to reach the summit quickly and safely.

Although everyone agrees that having a strong work ethic is important to achieve success and expertise, it is often unclear to them what a strong work ethic requires of them. In fact, it is a nice concept to think about, but not a lot of people actually work to make them a reality that they can live by. To most people, work ethics is just a pair of words that sound good but are not applied, despite the fact that it is essential in order to succeed.

The components for a strong work ethic

Timeliness is an important component of a strong work ethic. Being able to get things done in time as well as being punctual at work and meetings means you can stay on top of your work and business. Timeliness means you will be able to do everything that must be done in the time you set, keeping the stress levels low and the efficiency high.

Discipline is the ability to work or do what must be done despite any external and internal factors that say otherwise. Being a disciplined worker means getting things done once you set your mind to it because it is no longer subject to mood swings, erratic behavior, or convenience. Discipline will make sure that you get things done when they need to be done.

Professionalism is a standard that you have to get behind when it comes to how you conduct yourself toward your clients, your co-workers and your employers. And it's not just in how you treat others, but also in how you do your work and conduct business. Professionalism should be displayed as it is important for good working relationships and can be seen in work quality.

Balance is also a must when it comes to good work ethic. Balance in professional and personal life is important if you expect yourself to become a personal as well as a professional success. Balance means giving ample time for all aspects of your life, which also ensures quality of life and, in turn, quality of work.

Instilling a strong work ethic in yourself will shed a favorable light on you and your work, giving you more and more opportunities to grow and succeed as the people who work with you see how efficient and productive you handle your workload. A strong work ethic will make you a trustworthy addition to any company as it means you are a reliable worker who will do what needs to be done on time. You will become a pleasure to work with, for clients and co-workers alike, making you a far more valued individual within the workplace.

PRINCIPLE 22

GETTING INTO THE ZONE

There are instances when people work with such precision and expertise that time seems to slow down around them. Nothing occupies their mind other than their work and it takes up 100 percent of their mind. And before you know it, they have come up with the perfect solution, or managed to do something in half the time that would usually takes time to do. This is what most people refer to as "Getting into the Zone."

Getting into the zone is a level of concentration that beats them all. It reflects total absorption in a task that brings you to the highest level of enjoyment in your work. But getting into the zone is not always easy, and what worked for you before might not work for you again, which is why it's important to delve into what it takes to get into the zone.

What it takes

There has to be familiarity with the task

You have to be familiar with whatever it is you are doing, in fact, getting into the zone means not even trying anymore. An artist or poet might say the images or words just came to him, athletes say that they zone out. This means that it has to be something you can do without thinking, so much so that it becomes effortless at some point. It follows that you can't get into the zone when you're just learning to do something since you have to really think about it first.

Getting in the Zone involves the subconscious part of the brain and your emotions

As getting in the zone actually requires you to stop thinking about it, you have to let your subconscious take over. But you can never get into the zone when you're doing work that does not inspire you. When you are truly passionate about what you are doing, you can step out of your conscious mind and into the zone where you don't even have to think about what has to be done. But how do you tap your subconscious mind? Meditation and visualization exercises have been known to help in tapping the mind and getting you focused enough to enter your "zone", but there are other ways that can help as well. Listening to music is a great help. Athletes often train with music blaring in their ears. The effect of music on athletic performance has been well-documented, and additionally, music also helps in blocking out any distractions around you.

If you want to get into your zone, you must also make sure that you are in a place that is conducive to focusing and productivity. There are writers who swear by coffee shops, some who swear by parks or terminals; everyone has their own optimal environment. And don't forget that a healthy body and mind can find focus better than an unhealthy and exhausted one, so eat right, exercise, and get lots of sleep.

PRINCIPLE 23

STRENGTHEN YOUR WILLPOWER

Willpower, or self-control, is like a muscle that everyone has. There are those who exercise this muscle and get it stronger, to the point that flexing this muscle takes no effort, and their willpower is able to withstand even the strongest temptations. On the other hand, there are those who never exercise their willpower and give in to every temptation they face or desire that happens to fly by their minds. They end up having no self-control whatsoever.

Nowadays, as communication advances and information at your fingertips, instant gratification is the name of the game. If you want a pizza, you don't even have to go outside; you just pick up the phone and place an order. Added to this, you are constantly bombarded with advertisements that are designed to tempt you into buying things you had no intention of buying in the first place. Having no self-control can cause a lot of problems for you and even be the precursor to developing many more negative behaviors.

Keep track of your actions

A good way to exercise your willpower is by keeping a tab of your actions and not letting them get away with you. This means watching your words, your temper, and your negative tendencies. You might find that you are doing several things that have negative effects on your health or financial status. Imagine walking into a store to buy milk, and as you pass the food aisle, you end up buying cake mix, bacon, frozen pizza and ice cream on top of the milk. You're immediate desires got the better of you without you even realizing. Try to be observant of how you spend the day and what aspects you would like to improve on with regards to self-control.

Create a Routine

Willpower is finite. You can only control your impulses so much before you snap, and exhausting your energy on self-control can be stressful, and you have to find a way to augment this. When exercising or going to bed early is a struggle, don't worry, because the more you do it, the less of a struggle it becomes. Once you start developing routines that reinforce positive and healthy habits, it will become easier to do and won't take much willpower, which you can then exercise on other things.

Keep exercising, but don't exhaust yourself

Exercise your willpower muscle every day without exhausting your self-control stores. You can give in to the occasional cookie or sweets so that you can have the willpower to order a healthy salad for dinner rather than a cheeseburger and fries. As you continue to exercise this muscle, you will then have more self-control at your disposal. It is important to find balance in exercising your self-control without straining yourself too much.

Self-control is an admirable quality to have; it will allow you to take control of your baser desires as well as your own life. You will no longer be the victim of your own impulsive behavior. You can take your life in hand.

PRINCIPLE 24

FOSTERING DISCIPLINE

Discipline is an important quality that greatly benefits people in all aspects of life. It is discipline that will get you to keep going when things get tough, and it is discipline that will make you stick to your convictions and resolutions even if you're not in the mood or it is not convenient for you. Everyone recognizes the importance of discipline, but very few ever try to foster this quality in themselves.

Having a strong sense of self-discipline is a sign of great inner strength and will. It can be seen as your ability to keep the promises you make to yourself. When you say "I will not drink a drop of alcohol during weekdays," you are making a promise to yourself that you already know is worth keeping. With discipline, you can stick to your word and keep away from immediate gratification in order to reach a greater goal. Discipline is what will keep you going despite momentary setbacks and difficulties; it is what will make you persevere despite any hardships.

Discipline + Hard Work = Success

Contrary to what a lot of people think, it doesn't take a genius or innate brilliance in a certain field to become successful. In fact, those who are often considered geniuses are people who have constantly worked hard to attain the expertise and mastery needed to get to where they are. Even Mozart, a child genius, started training at a very young age and continued to develop his skills and talents until adulthood. In fact, thinking that all it takes is innate genius to succeed takes away from the people who work hard, stayed up late, and gave blood, sweat, and tears to achieve what they have. It is, in fact, discipline and hard work that is most needed in order to succeed and reach your goals, which means that you can be a master too, if you set your mind to it and foster discipline.

Self-Discipline vs. Vices

Discipline is also the quality that can keep you from vices that have the potential to harm your physical and mental health. It is self-discipline that can keep you from lighting up that "last" cigarette, or taking a bite off of that second burger. You can finally control your baser desires that you already know are bad for you. It is through self-discipline that you can finally get on track to becoming what you want to be.

Training for Discipline

A simple and yet effective way to train yourself to become more disciplined is by doing your tasks as soon as you can and not giving in to procrastination. Instead of waiting for the last minute before doing everything, set a time every day to work on those particular tasks. Try to do it a regular time so as to train your mind and body to anticipate the hour for your exercise, training etc.

Without instilling the quality of discipline into your life, plans will continue to remain just plans. It is discipline that will allow you to take timely action and improve your skill set with constant and regular practice. Discipline is important if you truly want to reach your goals.

PRINCIPLE 25

THE IMPORTANCE OF FOCUS AND MONOTASKING

A lot of people may think that multi-tasking, or doing two or three things at once, gets things done quicker, but that's not actually true. Doing two or more different actions at the same time can have a negative effect on how that task is done, in fact, you can end up doing poorly in all of them.

Why multitasking is a bad idea

The more you focus on a given task, the quicker it gets done and with much more quality. Although you might think that you are doing several things at the same time when you multitask, the truth is that you are actually splitting your time into tiny pieces and doing a little bit of everything in quick succession. Research has shown, however, that to really be absorbed in something, you need to spend considerably more time on it than just a few minutes (at least 10 minutes). Multitasking actually results in a slower pace and less quality of work than if you had just given the proper amount of time for each job.

The importance of focus

Focusing on a task means you are giving one hundred percent of your time and attention to getting the job or task done right. With focus, you will be able to finish the task quickly and effectively, and in far more creative way than if you were being distracted.

Focus means you can appreciate and interpret whatever it is you are doing, whether it's reading a book or trying to solve a certain problem. The decisive factor in getting a job done is not how much time is spent on it, but how much of your attention you devote to it. Focusing all your mental faculties into doing something means you can manage to finish it faster than if you had been distracted. Then, you can finally have extra time on your hands to do what you like with the added bonus that you have peace of mind because your chores are all done. When you focus your attention on something, you can rest assured that you have done and thought of everything you can and devoted yourself to that particular task.

Do it one after another

If you happen to have a lot on your plate, you already know that it's not a good idea to try and do more than one thing at a time. The best way to get through a long list of things to do is by making a list and ranking your tasks according to their urgency and importance, then doing one thing at a time in succession. This will ensure that you have focused and absorbed all aspects of each task, allowing you to solve and finish each to the best of your ability.

Once you allow yourself to focus on each task, you will find that you actually gain more time in your hands whilst the quality of your work also gets better. Focusing on your immediate tasks as well as your long-term goals is essential if you want to become successful.

PRINCIPLE 26

GIVE TIME TO NURTURE YOURSELF

The road to success is long and filled with difficulty, and it will take a lot of effort before you reach the summit, which is why it is important to give yourself a break every now and then in order to recharge and relax. Constantly working towards your goals without taking a break can cause you to burn out before even achieving them. Finding time for yourself to relax and enjoy life is just as important in achieving your goals as working hard and persevering. Taking the time out to enjoy and care for yourself should not be a guilty pleasure as it often seems to some, but an integral part of your day that can help you become more focused, energetic, and sharp in all aspects of your life.

The consequences of too much work

When every single day of your life is filled with financial records and bank statements, the world can seem like a rather grim and dull place (unless you happen to be a person who finds such things exciting). When you bury yourself in work, you have the very real threat of losing track of the simple joys and pleasures that make hardships and setbacks more bearable. Being in a constant state of nervousness or irritation will also have ill effects on your productivity, which can, in turn, become an extra source of stress. You have to set aside a little bit of time for yourself to regain optimal brain function and a positive outlook, which have been proven to greatly benefit your performance in the workplace.

Nurture your mind and body

You have to remember that your success relies on your well-being; you can't expect to reach your goals if you find yourself constantly stressed out, sick, or unhappy. Always remember to give yourself the time and opportunity to enjoy and relax, to pamper yourself and recharge after a long, stressful day. Set a date for reading a good book, or going out for a jog, you might even just give yourself 15 extra minutes in the bath for an extra relaxing soak, or 10 minutes every day for a walk through the park. No matter how simple the activity is, as long as you are sure to enjoy it, then it will serve to relax and energize you. Nurturing your body is just as important. You can do this by eating healthy, exercising, and avoiding any harmful practices. Treat your body well because it is the only one you've got, and the means by which you can reach your goals.

Treating yourself to these simple pleasures have enumerable benefits for your mental and physical well-being. Taking in the little pleasures relaxes your mind and will allow you to relieve tension that may have built up in your body. By giving yourself a break, you will be able to analyze the situation at work with fresh eyes and an energized brain, making it easier for you to come up with solutions or raise your productivity.

PRINCIPLE 27

YOU'LL ALWAYS NEED A STRONG SUPPORT SYSTEM

Man is a social animal in need of family and friends that take the journey of life along with him. Put a man in isolation and he turns feral, or simply loses his mind. But with a strong social network that supports and encourages him, man flourishes. Sometimes, the only other thing needed to achieve success is support. Having a strong support system of family and friends can give you the confidence and self-assurance to follow your dreams. Encouragement, love, and support are invaluable additions to anyone's tool belt.

If a support system is so important, it follows that you should value the people around you who truly love you and want the best for you. Know the people who truly want the best for you from those who are only fair weather friends. You have to know to value of those people in your life who also truly value you for who you are, regardless of success or failure.

You can get through anything with a strong support system

No matter how difficult life proves to be, no matter how many mistakes and regrets you end up having, when there are people around you who support you and believe in you, you can always get through and do better. Even though you are the one decisive in change and success in your life, having a support system will give you more courage to take risks and get through difficulty.

A healthy support system is not just beneficial in your personal life, it is important in personal matters as well. With a healthy support system, you know that there are people who will love you no matter what decisions you make or whom you choose to become. Family and friends will be the ones to help get you through the biggest personal problems, and they will also be right behind you, helping to push you towards your dreams

You will be happier

When you are surrounded by people who care and love you, the world seems like a brighter place. With loving people around you, you can become more positive and loving towards others around you. Knowing that you are loved and supported will make you more confident and able in every aspect of your life.

Maintain meaningful relationships

There are plenty of people who reach a point in their lives where they look around and don't really find any of the loving support that they need. They have none of the healthy relationships they once had, they do not get support from family, or even their spouses. This mostly means that at some point, there was a breakdown in communication and love. How can you keep this from happening? Simple, by being open, honest, and appreciative.

Let them know that they are important, and that you are thankful to have them in your life. Listen to them when they give you advice and go out of your way to reach out.

PRINCIPLE 28

THE SIGNIFICANCE OF EMOTIONAL INTELLIGENCE

Emotional intelligence pertains to your ability to understand other people's emotions, the ability to sympathize and empathize with them, and understanding their reactions, as well as being confident and in control of yourself. These are all attributes that can help you achieve success. Your emotional intelligence dictates how well you can get along, understand, and get other people to understand you. Emotional intelligence is important for succeeding in the workplace and succeeding in life in general.

E.I. in your personal life

Being emotionally intelligent is what allows you to relate to others and at the same time make yourself relatable. How high your emotional intelligence is has a direct effect on how you treat others and how you present yourself to others in a way that is favorable, because with high emotional intelligence, you are able to perceive and understand your own actions as well as those around you. Having low EI or EQ has been shown to have a correlation in bullying, as both bullies and victims of bullying were found to have relatively low scores with regards to emotional intelligence, as they are unable to fully process the destructiveness of such acts on themselves and the other person.

Research has shown that having high emotional intelligence means you are able to have better relationships, better reasoning and people skills, as well as more confidence and higher self-esteem. It also makes you more endearing, trustworthy, and friendly to other people, which means that emotionally intelligent people tend to have better socializing skills and more friends.

E.I. in the workplace means synergy

When everyone in the workplace shows strong emotional intelligence, i.e. they are supportive and considerate of each other and are working together in harmony, it makes the wheels of business run along more smoothly. When someone has high emotional intelligence, it means that he or she can work well with other people and are more open to change and adjustments in work style. They are able to deal with co-workers and clients better and foster strong ties with them, making the atmosphere within the workplace one of easy camaraderie.

Having an *organization* that is emotionally intelligent is even better. It means that everyone is motivated by and supportive of each other. Everyone becomes highly efficient and committed to the work because they perceive themselves as part of the greater whole, which also increases their productivity. An organization that is emotionally intelligent becomes more than the sum of its parts. They can work with initiative and will be able to deal with problems together as a collective. Those who work in the managerial department or in sales and marketing need emotional intelligence to become successful in their professions.

The good thing about Emotional Intelligence is that it can be learned as time goes on. You can train your mind to becoming more empathetic and sensitive towards your own feelings and that of others. This means that you can start learning E.I. skills that are sure to get you far.

> "BY LEARNING TO UTILIZE THE POWER OF OUR THOUGHTS, BOTH POSITIVE AND NEGATIVE, WE WILL CONTINUOUSLY DO THE TASKS NEEDED TO ACHIEVE GREATNESS."

"Are You just going through the motions?"

PRINCIPLE 29

DEVELOPING PROFESSIONALISM

Professionalism is the conduct and qualities that a skilled professional or someone in a specialized occupation should imbue. But what are these qualities and conducts anyway? How do you know if you are acting the way a professional ought to act?

Have the necessary skills and knowledge

In order to be considered a true professional, you have to have all the specialized skills and the proper knowledge of your field. A professional makes a commitment to his chosen profession, a commitment to continue to learn and improve his craft, and add to his knowledge. Even though different professions have different requirements when it comes to levels of knowledge, skill sets, and academic training, being a professional still means that you continue to do your work with dedication and earnestness, that you continue to learn, whether it's at the factory floor, workshop, office, or training center.

Honesty, Competency, and Accountability

A true professional is someone that employers, co-workers, and clients can trust. He, or she, can be trusted to do his work well and with integrity, to do the best he can to achieve set goals and plans, and to take responsibility for the outcome of his words or actions. You have to be honest with the people you work with or for, and develop trust. This requires being competent in your work and also being honest and accountable in your actions. You have to be able to own up if you make a mistake or do something wrong. This will show everyone around you that you are a true professional who does not shy away from responsibility and is someone that can be trusted.

Treat people with respect and carry yourself with dignity

You have to be respectful and polite when handling clients, interacting with co-workers, and communicating with employers. This is a true sign of professionalism. You have to treat people with respect no matter who they are, whether they stand below or above you. This quality not only defines a true professional, but is also a sign of someone of good character.

Another thing to remember is to look and act the part of a true professional. Dress yourself well and carry yourself in a dignified manner. In other words, you can simply exude professionalism by the way you act and carry yourself. Try to dress smartly and conduct yourself with dignity, make your actions command respect. Dressing well and having good manners not only speaks of how you want to be perceived but also how you value those around you. Being polite and well groomed means that the views, comfort, and opinions of those around you count; it means that you realize that they deserve to be treated to the best side of you.

Professionalism manifests itself in your output and your conduct in the workplace. Make sure that you are prepared with the knowledge needed to do your job well and, at the same time, foster relationships within the workplace that comprises of mutual respectful and admiration.

PRINCIPLE 30

DEVELOPING COMPETENCE IN YOURSELF AND OTHERS

No matter where you are in life, you must continue to improve and develop. Not just in a personal sense, but with your skills and talents as well. Realizing one's true potential is a very real and natural human desire, and nothing causes regret more than having a certain talent or skill left unexplored. Being competent in something is a basic human need that makes a person feel that they are a valued and productive member of society.

Competence at Work

Continuing to develop your skills and talents, whether they fall within the sphere of the workplace or not, can be a great source of fulfillment and personal satisfaction, as well as open up new opportunities to you as you gain mastery over them. Becoming highly skilled at something is one of the 3 basic human needs within the scope of self-determination theory. It is stated that competence and confidence in doing a certain task, knowing that you are skilled and valued in your work, is something everyone needs so they can be a well-rounded person. When you are confident in your skills and capabilities, you become more daring and creative when solving problems or coming up with new techniques that bring added value to your company or workplace.

Gaining Competence

Of course, in order to gain competence, you have to continue working on your skills and talents. Hard-work is always the first ingredient if you want to be really great at something. No matter how good you already think you are, know that you can still get better. Always be open to learning. As long as you keep your mind open to learning more, you will never fall behind. On the other hand, thinking that you've already learned everything you need to learn will make your mind closed off to more knowledge and training. There will no longer be room to grow.

Helping others gain competence

Doesn't it feel nice when you are told that you did a good job? Doesn't knowing that you are valued and appreciated make you want to work harder and be better? No matter how good you are in the workplace, you will always need the help and support of your co-workers or employees in order to achieve success, and making them gain competence is a great way of upping productivity and camaraderie in the workplace. Continued training and skill development benefits everyone, and outward shows of appreciation can help foster strong ties and better work ethics within the workplace. You can tell your co-workers or employees, even your boss that you think they did a great job and it is a pleasure working with them. Let others know that you appreciate them and soon, they will show you appreciation.

The knowledge that one is competent in their profession is always a great feeling, one that encourages further growth and learning. It is an important aspect of living a full and satisfying life that will make you feel valuable and valued within the workplace.

"Don't wait for success to come to you. Be proactive to ensure that you attain the success you desire."

"If you lived an average day, every day, for the next 5 years, what is the logical outcome?"

PRINCIPLE 31

LEARN TO LISTEN

There is not a day that goes by without you having a conversation with someone, but what is the quality of the conversation? There are times when a conversation is hardly an exchange at all. It has become quite easy to actually end up with a monologue instead of a dialogue when going into conversations. Many people want the comfort of being able to express themselves and get their ideas out there without giving a thought on what the other person is trying to say. They can be so engrossed in what they are thinking that what the other person says hardly makes a difference at all. You have to learn to deliver and receive ideas and opinions in order for you to create real human connections that enrich your life as well as be more successful in life.

You can never go far on your own. No matter how brilliant you are, you will always need the help and trust of others in order to get far. This is why listening is such an important skill to learn. Listening properly allows you to empathize, understand, and learn more effectively. When you listen, you are no longer stuck in your own perceptions, instead, your mind is broadened through the words of another as they share their opinions, views, and knowledge with you.

The HEAR technique

The hear technique is a guide that teachers often give their students in order to understand and learn better, but it is a technique that can be used in social and professional interactions as well. Following this technique will help you to internalize and respond well when it comes to having dialogues, meetings, and receiving instructions.

Halt. If you really want to take in what another person is saying, stop whatever it is that you are doing and give them your full attention. This means doing away with distractions and clearing any inner dialogue you may be having.

Engage. Face the speaker to show that you are listening and focus on what they have to say. Show them that you care and want to understand, at the same time, having your body in attention will allow your mind to follow suit more easily.

Anticipate. Anticipate what the speaker intends to say next. This allows you to point your mind toward what is being said rather than getting distracted.

Replay. Run what was just said through your head again and analyze it. You can have discussions with your co-workers or staff and have a lively give and take on the merits and disadvantages of the ideas that were shared. This will ensure that you have truly internalized the information.

Learning to listen is an important skill that will bring you far in life. Listening means you can forge stronger ties with the people around you, enriching your personal life, and at the same time, you'll be able to have a clear understanding of what your clients and employers want and need, also enriching your professional life.

PRINCIPLE 32

HUMAN CONNECTIONS

Another basic human need is forming deep and meaningful connections with others. Man is a social being, and the need for social interactions is essential to living a fulfilling life.

In the age of the internet, it seems as if connections have gotten stronger, as it has become easier to send messages, and let everyone know what you are doing. But are these real connections that satisfy your need for relatedness, kinship, support, and understanding? More often than not, these "digital connections" are just that and extend no farther than your phone or pc. But to be clear, not all digital connections are superficial, there are people who gain confidence and develop true friendships through the relationships they create on the internet. It all comes down to the quality of the connections.

Quality connections

How do you know if you have quality connections? Simple, do you treat each other with respect and kindness? Do you value each other's opinions? Do you support each other in making decisions? This is how you measure true human connections, through mutual support, affection, and respect. A person may interact with a certain number of people a day, they may even go to parties every weekend and have thousands of followers on Facebook, Instagram, and Twitter, but, despite all these, still there are no real human connections.

Developing Quality Connections at Work and at Play

When you treat people poorly, you will make them respond to you poorly as well. If you demean their work and lose patience with them, you cannot expect encouragement and support, but you can expect to be ignored and alienated from your co-workers. A negative experience in the workplace will bring about negative results in work as well, no matter how brilliant or skilled a person may be. Having quality human connections in the work place has proven to have a strong effect in productivity and efficiency. With human connections, you start to love your job, and work is no longer just work, it becomes a source of professional and social satisfaction.

But how do you create strong social connections at work? The answer is by treating people with kindness, consideration, and respect. Think about how you would like to be treated and try to project that idea into how you treat others around you. It is important that you continue to work on your relationships and treat people in the way that they deserve to be treated, at the same time, make sure that the relationships you maintain are with people who truly value and appreciate you for who you are. Quality connections go both ways after all, and you can't just let yourself turn into a doormat for someone who doesn't realize your worth as a person.

As you develop quality connections with the people around you, you will notice an enhanced sense of well-being and satisfaction in your life. Having a good support system can help enhance your confidence to make important decisions and risks, and give you the fortitude to get through problems.

PRINCIPLE 33

WHY YOU SHOULD LIVE WITH LOVING KINDNESS

Loving kindness is more of a spiritual practice of treating people with kindness that is fueled with love. It is a deeply spiritual and satisfying principle to live by and is the foundation for many religions. But you don't have to be active in a church, temple, or synagogue in order to understand and practice loving kindness in your daily life.

Bringing a world view of loving kindness into your life requires some meditation time, but it is easy and simple and can be done whenever and wherever you want. All it takes is quiet time and the right intentions. In meditation, intentions are always important. Why do you want to look inside yourself? What do you want to achieve? The important thing here is that your intentions are on the right track, i.e. you want a heart filled with kindness and love for all things around you. It may seem corny, but this is a deeply spiritual practice that has many physical and mental benefits for you.

You will learn to love yourself and wish yourself well

In practicing loving kindness, you want to feel love for all around you, but you have to love yourself before you can project this love to others. The meditation often starts with counting breaths and clearing the mind, once you manage that, it is time to let your wishes for yourself rise to the surface of your mind. Allow positive thoughts for yourself drift up, examples would be "I wish to be well," "I wish to be happy," "I wish to be kind," "I wish to be loved," and so on. Let these thoughts fill your heart with well-wishes and positivity. Through this exercise, you will be positive and kind to yourself in ways that you might not have been before.

You will learn to direct loving kindness towards others

Once you feel and internalize this love and kindness directed at yourself, you can turn your attention to another person. You can start saying the same phrases in the second person and with a person you care for. Send the loving kindness their way with an open heart filled with love. Once this becomes easier for you, you can start visualizing someone you are familiar with but don't know personally, it could be someone you notice on the same bus every morning, or someone you notice as you walk by heading to your office. The next step would be to send this loving kindness towards those you don't like or even have arguments with. Think of them and wish them well. As you continue to do this every day, you can widen your scope until you can send love to all beings on earth light-heartedly.

Practicing loving kindness in everyday life is a deeply healing and profound experience. With loving kindness, you will only have positivity and goodwill in your heart and mind, leaving you free from negative emotions that trap and stunt your personal growth.

PRINCIPLE 34

STAYING HUMBLE

Humility is one of the most important virtues that anyone can have, and it was once greatly valued in the society, yet nowadays, it is often forgotten. Social media caters to the superficial and narcissistic side of society, and everyone is becoming more and more obsessed with outward appearances and flashy shows of wealth. The truth is that it is becoming harder and harder to find signs of humility in the world. But why is it important to be humble and how does that benefit you in a world where everyone wants to flaunt their success?

Humility however, has been proven to have many benefits to the human mind as well as being evidence of good character. Humility means being able to know your own limitations and who you are in relation to the world as a whole. It means you don't live inside your own head and that you are not preoccupied only with yourself. Humility is evidence of a broad world view as well as higher intelligence.

Being humble means being aware of yourself and your mortality

Humility means that you are able to see your own weaknesses along with your strengths. You realize that the world doesn't revolve around you and that you are just a small part in the grand scheme of things. Unlike other people who hide behind flamboyant shows of wealth and beauty, you know that wealth and beauty do not define you or make you better than others and you can carry this view on to how you see others.

Humility makes you easier to deal with

If you remain humble despite great successes, it makes you easier to deal with and work with. People will be able to approach you and talk to you without having to go through the steel doors of arrogance. If you hold a leadership position, humility will not only make you more likable among the people who work for you, it will also make you a more effective leader. As a leader, humility will allow you to see the strengths in others, admit to any mistakes you may have made, and be adaptable to the needs of those who work for you.

Humility means that you harbor less prejudice

People who have no humility tend to have an exaggerated sense of entitlement, making them hold certain prejudiced views when it comes to their beliefs. This also makes them less tolerant of others who are different or strange in their view. Being humble, on the other hand, means that you are aware that there are others with different practices and beliefs as you, and you're okay with that because you realized that the world is a big place and everyone has their place in it.

Humility may be a virtue that is going out of style, but it is also one that should be valued all the more. The world will be such a better place if people exhibited a bit more humility, and what come with it: empathy, sensitivity, and tolerance.

PRINCIPLE 35

AN ATTITUDE FOR HAPPINESS

A person can be rich and famous, with every single one of their needs and wants catered to and still be unhappy and frustrated with life, while there are those who go through hardships that others can't even imagine, much less endure, and still wake up every morning with a smile on their faces. Why do you think this is so?

It's not about Material Possessions

Acquiring wealth and social status do not necessarily mean happiness, if it were then life would be much simpler. Nowadays, people have been taught, through media, education and entertainment, that getting rich or becoming famous are the most important things for you to finally "make it" in the world, but many people actually lose their chances of ever being happy because of this. When life is measured by the wealth you gain, you often end up forgetting to live. A vast majority of people go through life always hurrying from one place to the next, from one appointment or meeting to another, all in the hopes of closing that deal, making that acquisition, thinking that those will make them happy. But more often than not, this constant race to achieve goals and meet deadlines end up keeping them from actually making the memories and personal connections that make life worth living. Isn't it sad when, in the search for fulfillment, people end up living empty lives?

It's not about indulgence

Indulging in gratification and pleasures can bring some sense of satisfaction, but it never really lasts, and before long, you find yourself with that empty feeling again, and searching for the next surge of pleasure. Indulging in pleasures can make you happy, but it can never give you the sense of well-being and satisfaction in life that constitutes true happiness.

True Happiness

So where does true happiness reside? You need look no further than in yourself, because happiness isn't supposed to be sought in far off lands, or at the bottom of treasure chests, happiness is rediscovered within yourself. In order to find happiness in your life, you don't need to do more than foster an attitude that is open and embraces all aspects of your life in a positive way. How you view your life, no matter how difficult it seems, is all that matters, and your attitude toward difficulties, problems and trials, determines how you end up coping with them. Having an attitude of positivity and fostering a sense of well-being will allow you to get one step closer to finding true happiness, happiness that does not rely on material things or those of temporary pleasure.

Having the right attitude towards life will allow you to find true happiness within you, and this will allow you to grow and enjoy life as you live it. It is happiness that will allow you to reach for your goals with creativity and motivation rather than grim routine, happiness that can drive you to find your true passion and live your life without doubt, fear or regret.

PRINCIPLE 36

BENG THANKFUL

Fostering an attitude of thankfulness and appreciation is a central part of gaining mastery over your own life and achieving your goals with optimism, and at the same time, enjoying and cherishing your life as it is now.

Having an attitude of thankfulness means being aware of all the blessings that you already have rather than focusing on what is missing in your life. An attitude that is sorely missing in many people nowadays. Consumerism in today's modern culture has taught people to want things they don't need, to bury whatever unhappiness or dissatisfaction they feel in their lives by accumulating possessions that can never give them the sense of satisfaction that they are looking for.

Take a look around

One of the easiest ways to develop an attitude of thankfulness is by stopping to smell the roses. The idiom basically means taking time out to appreciate the beauty of life and it's something that a lot of people have to learn to do. Everything in the 21st century is happening so fast. Technological advances are being brought forth every day, trends and fads change overnight, new products, new plans, new people come and go in the blink of an eye in the post-modern world, and it becomes easy to lose track of what is important. However, if you keep in mind that you want to relish life, you can surely take some time every day to reflect on the good things in life and focus your thoughts on what you should be thankful for.

Never compare

There will always be someone who has more or less of something, or is better or worse at something than you, and comparing yourself and your life to that of others can only cause you to either be prideful and vain, or dissatisfied and frustrated. Realize that everyone is different, and everyone is unique. Everyone lives their lives according to their personal views and standards and to achieve success, you only need to out do only yourself and no one else.

Be aware of your blessings

No matter who you are and what your situation is, surely there is something in your life that makes you smile, that fills you with pride, that make you feel all warm and fuzzy inside. It doesn't matter if it's something simple or silly; after all, blessings aren't always grandiose. Be thankful for everything you have, and if you think you have nothing to be thankful for then just be thankful for LIFE. Be thankful for being able to feel and breathe, for being able to dance or sing, for having the opportunity to love and be loved. Appreciate the fact that there are people in your life who value and cherish you simply because you're you and there's no one else like you.

No matter how simple it is, acknowledge it and let it fill your heart with joy. Remind yourself every day that life is worth living simply for what it is and that every moment is a gift that should be cherished.

PRINCIPLE 37

WHY IT'S A GOOD IDEA TO BE FRUGAL

When you find yourself getting a good promotion with a significant pay-raise, or even just getting a well-paying job for the first time, one of your first impulses would be to splurge on yourself and the people you love, and although this can be fun once in a while, make sure to set some money aside. Live within your means and surely, you will never want. It is imperative that you exercise the virtue of frugality.

It can be so easy to find new things to spend money on. In fact, people are being programmed toward consumerism with the proliferation of commercials, ads, and celebrities all selling something. But allowing your money to fly out of your hands at the store can cause many problems for you, not to mention falling into debt can be a very difficult hole to climb out of. Therefore, it is always wise to exercise prudence when it comes to expenses.

Don't over stretch your income

Make sure to keep your expenses at a level that you can sustain. Weigh the important expenses that you have to make against the more frivolous ones. If you find your budget getting depleted before the end of the month, review your expenses and make cuts when you can. For example, if you find that you only have a couple hundred dollars left after all your expenses have been taken into account; it would be time to cut back on certain things.

Rank your expenses according to importance. Make sure to take everything into account, including possible emergencies, so that you have a clear picture of where your finances stand.

When it comes to writing down your income, don't include money you may or may not end up getting, such a bonus that hasn't arrived yet, or tips you may or may not get. Write down only the regular amount of money that you are sure to receive. You can't account for something that isn't there yet.

Set a little bit aside every month

Having savings will help you greatly. Make sure you set aside money in case there's an accident or emergency. This way, you can be assured that you'll never really be flat out broke. This will give you peace of mind and security.

Consume less

Truth be told, most people buy so much and have it end up going to waste. There are men and women who have closets full of clothes they've only worn once like 5 years ago. Tons and tons of food go to waste every year in the United States, and all for what? People have been programmed to buy before thinking, not realizing how wasteful it is and how bad it is for the environment, as the earth only has a limited amount of resources.

Living frugally will keep you safe from debts and deficits, with the added assurance of savings to use for emergencies or for the future. You will surely rest easy knowing that your finances are all in order.

PRINCIPLE 38

THE SECRETS TO RISK-TAKING IN BUSINESS

It is often said that to win big, you have to take big risks, like the saying that goes, "You have to risk it to get the biscuit," meaning that you'll only get big rewards when you make big risks, but there is a method to what seems like the madness of taking risks. Although making risks can come with big rewards, you have to realize that risk-taking has to serve a purpose, or better yet, take calculated risks that have the odds in your favor.

The current business models popular nowadays say that in order for you to succeed, you need to be a risk-taker and not afraid to put yourself out there, and many business people consider having failed at least once as a badge of honor. But not all risks are worth taking, and risk-taking doesn't always work out well for everyone. Below are a few simple tips you should follow when thinking about taking risks.

- Make it a Strategic risk. Although you are taking chances when making a risk, it should never be a rash decision that serves no purpose. Make sure that every risk you take has a function and can add value to your company. This means that you have to make them strategic risks that you know will eventually pay off for your company.

- You have to be ready to take a loss. Taking a risk means that you have to be open to failure and losses. When you take a risk, make sure you don't put everything out there right away as that could cripple your company or business. Taking a huge financial risk with a relatively new company is never wise, so try to take risks that you know you can get through even if you do fail, and remember that even if you figure in some losses in the beginning, it can still pay off in the end.

- Risk doesn't come cheap. Taking risks, especially when testing out a new idea or business scheme, can come at a pretty steep price, and you have to be aware of just what that price is. Find out how much it will take and how much you can realistically spend without losing your business or your employees. Make a financial plan for your risk-taking and do your best to stick to it.

- You need to be patient. Some of the risks you are taking now can take months or even years before they pay off. You have to be aware of this and factor it in when it comes to your business. Sometimes, the risks you are taking might not even yield any financial return at all, so make sure you know what you are expecting when you make these risks and figure out if they're worth it, as these kinds of risks can be a big challenge for small businesses.

The trick to taking risks is analyzing it as best as you can. Make sure your projections are realistic and make sure you don't over-reach.

PRINCIPLE 39

DEVELOP EFFECTIVE TIME MANAGEMENT SKILLS

Time is the only resource that can never be earned back once it is spent, which is why it is so important to manage time wisely and not let a single second go to waste. Every person on earth has the same amount of time every day that they can spend on being productive, being creative, or being at rest. How time is spent relies solely on the individual, and since it is such an important resource, it follows that one must give careful consideration on how individual time is allocated during the day, month, year, and even lifetime.

When you find yourself always running out of time, whether it is regarding punctuality when getting to work, meeting deadlines, or simply being unable to do any chores at home because you are always too busy, then you need to start developing time management skills.

Divide your time amongst important and essential tasks

Time management is a skill set that will allow you to better allocate the time that you have so that you never end up racing against time. With time management, time becomes your ally; you will never have to race against time. With proper time management, you can divide your time properly amongst the different tasks that you need to get done throughout the day in a more structured and focused manner, getting them done quickly and efficiently.

Time management for success

Time management can pave the way to success. When you manage your time properly, you will be able to give time to different aspects of your personal and professional development. Once you get the hang of dividing your time efficiently, you will be able to give time to developing skills, improving work efficiency, and managing to have more time left for personal enjoyment and relaxation. Managing your time efficiently means that you will actually gain more free time to do other things or to get ahead on your workload.

A simple way to manage your time

There are many different ways to manage your time, but the easiest is to simply make a time table for all the things you need to do for the day, week, and month. This will help give you a better idea of all the things you need to do and allocate time so as not to lose track of any of them. It often happens that because there are so many different tasks that need to be done, one or two slip through the cracks and are forgotten, which then ends up coming back to haunt you when the deadline looms or the consequences become evident. But if you keep a detailed list of what has to be done, you will not lose track of anything, and gain peace of mind.

Through proper time management, you will find your days to be full and fruitful with more free time in your hands to relax and shake off the stress. This is a sure-fire skill that leads to success and happiness!

PRINCIPLE 40

THE BENEFITS OF EXERCISE

Along with a healthy diet, one needs a good amount of exercise in order to stay healthy. Your body is a machine designed to serve for whatever purpose you need. Letting your body grow weak through idleness is a big waste of a miraculous product of evolution. Your body is a miracle in itself and is capable of doing nearly anything if you take care and work for it.

The Benefits of Exercise

Exercising hold many benefits for your mind and body. Exercising lowers your blood pressure, strengthens your heart, and can help you maintain a healthy body weight and combat obesity. Your body has evolved to run and fight in the plains, deserts, and forests of the world. Your body is supposed to exert and sweat in order to be in optimal health. The sedentary lifestyle that society has developed is causing a huge portion of the population to suffer different types of ailments that can easily be prevented by making certain lifestyle changes. Diabetes, hypertension, and obesity are all ailments taking over a huge portion of the population despite the fact that all these can be avoided with just a bit more self-control and exercise.

Exercise also has beneficial effects on the mind. It has been scientifically proven that going out to do some exercise every day gives you better mental stability, as well as making you happier and positive in daily life. Exercising increases the production of dopamine and serotonin, which is associated with a happier disposition. Exercise has also been effectively used as part of the therapy to treat depression, as well as lower the chances of suffering from anxiety and panic attacks. All in all, exercise strengthens all aspects of a person. You become stronger physically and mentally through exercise.

Find exercise that is enjoyable for you

A lot of people have a concept of exercise that is mostly negative, and the image of yourself sweating at a treadmill trying to catch your breath can be enough to make you have second thoughts about exercise. But there is a way around this that is quite simple - find an exercise style that you can enjoy. Do you like dancing? Then opt for an exercise regimen that involves that, there's Zumba, hip-hop dancing, or ballroom dancing. If you like playing football then you can organize a game with your friends every week, or practice on your own in the backyard. You don't have to go to the gym or try those vigorous and difficult exercises, all that matters is you sweat it out and get your heart rate up for at least half an hour. You can even play Wii games that involve a lot of movement in your living room and it can already be considered a form of exercise. Remember not to shock your body and go about it slowly but regularly.

Exercise already offers so many benefits that it's a wonder why people have to be convinced themselves just to do it. In the end, you will only have gains to your overall health and happiness with regular exercise.

PRINCIPLE 41

EATING HEALTHY

Your physical body is essential to you. It is with your physical body that you set out to do all the things you want to do. It is with your physical body that you can launch your career, help others, and gain success. Your body is the temple of your mind and spirit, and you have to make sure you keep it in good working condition in order to preserve it and maximize your capabilities.

You have to treat your body right if you expect to do a lot more in your future. It is important that you always keep your health in mind and not give in to certain vices that can potentially harm your health and well-being. Living an unhealthy lifestyle can greatly limit what you can achieve, and can even become a constant source of suffering for you. Doing right to your body is the same as treating yourself well, something that you should always strive to do.

Give yourself nourishment, not junk

Having a healthy diet is essential to your overall health, and it is often in this basic aspect that many people fail. Unhealthy food line the streets, and there isn't a highway or street corner that doesn't at least have one fast food outlet or grocery store that sells junk food, soda, and other very unhealthy food. In fact, people encounter more high-fat and high-sugar foods than organic, fresh produce in everyday life. Junk food and fast food have the benefit of convenience, as they are cheap and easy to cook, but the long-term and short-term ill effects more than outweigh whatever convenience or instant gratification they might offer. You might say that following a strict diet is something that just seems impossible for you, but you don't have to fall into a diet to eat healthily. It simply means that you are eating the right amount from all the different food groups. Also, eating healthier can be as simple as checking the labels and nutritional values. Make sure the food is low on trans-fat, sugars, and sodium, the main causes of lifestyle diseases. Also, make sure you have more fruits and vegetables in your daily food intake than anything else.

Do it because YOU are worth it

When someone gets a new car, they want to take care of it and keep it in good condition. They would buy the right kind of fuel and treat it well so that it will always look new. If people would do this for a car, a house, or whatever equipment they have, then why not for the body, which is truly irreplaceable.

There is the old expression "You are what you eat," which continues to hold true. What you put into your body reflects how you value yourself and your health. Why would you keep eating garbage if you do not consider your body a trash can? Eating healthy and watching your diet means you value yourself and your life. It means that you recognize the importance of your own health.

PRINCIPLE 42

SLEEP

Many people start the day being tired. They wake up feeling stressed out and exhausted no matter how much time they spend in bed, which probably means that there's something wrong with their sleep patterns. Sleep is vital for a healthy mind and body, just as food is, but so many people don't really give sleep its dues. Without sleep, your mind becomes a dark and scary place and you can go crazy from lack of sleep as your body suffers the stress, too. You have to find the right sleeping cycle that can give you energy to get through the day and get on top of the things you need to do. Here are a few tips on how to achieve optimal sleeping hours.

Start a routine

Setting up your internal clock is important. You have to have a certain pattern every day. Develop the habit of going and getting out of bed at the same time every day. Developing a routine will acquaint your body to the pattern, and as time passes, you will find yourself ready for bed at the same time every day, and up and about at approximately the same time as well. Try to stick to this pattern as much as you can so that you can at least have a starting point for when you optimize the number of hours you sleep.

Customize your pattern

Everyone has their own needs when it comes to sleep. There are people who can't get by with less than 8 hours, while others are perfectly happy with just 7, and others need at least 9 hours.

Everyone is built differently and has their individual needs to be fulfilled. You can find out your optimal sleeping routine by starting with 7 hours of sleep. If you find that you are still tired in the morning, try to go to bed 30 minutes earlier than you did the night before but get up at the same time. Do you feel more rested than the night before or are you still a little tired? If so, you can keep going, go to bed another 30 minutes earlier and see how you feel when you wake up the next day. Is it better? Continue to do this to the point when you find yourself most rested in the mornings.

Relax and calm your mind and body

Going to bed as a bundle of nerves can make it difficult for you to sleep and leave you still feeling frazzled in the morning. You have to take the time to relax yourself before going to bed. One of the best ways to do this is by taking a hot bath before bed. Relax yourself in the bath for as long as you need so that you can go to bed and sleep in a state of calm. You should also turn off all your electronic gadgets so that your mind is without distractions, but only mindless information that you don't really need.

You have to make sure that you get enough sleep. Make sure that you feel rested in the morning so that there is more of the world that you can take on!

PRINCIPLE 43

WHY SPIRITUALITY MATTERS

Why do people need spirituality and what is it anyway? Is it participating in religious practices? Is it about adopting a specific faith? These are question that are often asked when it comes to spirituality, and rightly so. There are so many blurry lines when it comes to understanding spirituality that it is pretty easy to make mistakes or get confused.

Spirituality is about finding a deeper meaning to life, about getting connected to the earth, to nature, and to other people through the search for answers to the unknown. Unlike what most people believe, spirituality is not about bowing down to what is considered the "right" faith; developing spirituality is deeply personal and should answer your unique needs when it comes to finding answers in your life. How you develop spiritual and through which medium are decisions that are solely up to you and should not be subject or vulnerable to public opinion.

Adds quality to your life

Finding spirituality is a wondrous journey in itself. The world is filled with religions and faiths with teaching that may or may not resonate with you. Going to a church or temple mechanically simply because you were raised that way is not real spirituality. The faith that you have should move you and touch your life in a deep and personal level. Spirituality should add to the meaning and quality of your life. Through spirituality, you can find meaning, order, and peace in a world of chaos. Through spiritual experiences, you will be able to resolve the sufferings and difficulties of life with something that is bigger and greater than you, as well as bring you closer to people who have the same faith and beliefs as yourself.

It can help you be better and brings you comfort

The belief that there is something sacred in the world, something beyond man call, help people try to be the best that they can be. When you believe that there is something infinitely good in the world, then you are able to believe that there is something infinitely good in you as well.

Developing spirituality in your life can bring many comforts as long as you retain how personal this journey should be. There are those who find meaning in the belief that something, or someone, greater than them is directing life, that everything is happening for a reason. There are others who believe that the best that can happen is to find peace in the midst of chaos, to find peace within themselves. Everyone has their own leanings and beliefs, their own needs that they can fill by incorporating spirituality into their lives.

Be tolerant of others

Always remember how you discovered spirituality, not religion. Remember how deeply meaningful and touching it was for you, and, especially, how personal it was. There are those who may not believe in what you believe in, but recognize that that is their choice. They may have found meaning in their lives in their own way, just as you have.

PRINCIPLE 44

THE STRENGTH OF AFFIRMATIONS

Everyone has faults and weaknesses that they want to change or improve in themselves, but changing yourself for the better is often easier said than done. Affirmations are a great way to get through to yourself and make use of your innate potential. With positive and active statements, you can effectively condition yourself to change or improve certain aspects of your personality or habits.

The best way to go about using affirmations is by writing them for yourself. No one knows you better than you and the more specific the affirmations are, the more effective they will be. Don't worry if you find that some of them have to be altered. This is totally fine. Tweaking your affirmations to better suit your particular needs make them more effective.

Start with personal reflections

Before you start writing your affirmations, you have to spend some time looking inward. You have to find specific areas in your life that you want to alter. To do this, you need to spend time on serious reflection. Clear your mind and focus your thoughts on what you want to change or improve. You can also consider observations that others may have made about you that hit home. It would be good idea to make a list of these factors and to analyze them together. See if you can find a recurring theme. It could be specific, such as the desire for validation from others, or broad, such as being unworthy of love.

Writing your affirmations

Once you have found the main points that you want to change, you can start writing your affirmations. There are some basic rules in writing your affirmations. They have to be written in the present tense, in the first person (and they should also be deeply personal to you) and should be attainable. This means you probably should not say "I will never…" if you do not think it is easily attainable. Affirmations should be positive and empowering, implying active resolution, so if you think you might be impatient, you can say "I am willing to wait." Make sure that the affirmations you are writing truly resonate and have a deep effect on you. Better quality over quantity, as writing a few but hard hitting affirmations can help you focus on those aspects more, which in turn, makes the affirmations more effective.

Using your Affirmations

Say these affirmations to yourself at least twice a day every day. It is a good idea to say them when you wake up in the morning and get up from bed. This way, you can start the day with the affirmations already in your heart. Feel your body as you speak these affirmations and try to notice where the effects lay. This will help you focus on the effects of the affirmation more strongly.

Using affirmations is a simple and easy way to improve yourself effectively with only your reflections and will power. Affirmations are helpful in a way that you can speak of only positive things that you want to occur in your life and trust that you can make them happen.

PRINCIPLE 45

CHOOSING LOVE

When it comes to life, you always have the choice. You can choose to go one way or the other. You can choose to work for money, or make money work for you, you can choose to live with positivity, or you can choose to be negative, every emotion you feel every day is a choice you make, whether consciously or unconsciously.

Similarly, you can choose to live with fear in your heart, or you can choose to live with love. This doesn't mean romantic love, but love for yourself and for all things in general. When you fear something, you can't get to know it, you can't appreciate it, and you can't work around it. You form negative and sometimes unfounded opinions about it that keep you from growing. But living with encompassing love for yourself and all things give you a sense of wellness, assurance and positivity that lifts you up and away from suffering.

Fear paralyses

If you fear something, such as the future or the consequences of a mistake, etc., you end up seeing only that thing which you fear. You might end up thinking that there is no way to get around it, that there is nothing you can do. But if you knew to dispel the fear, you would realize that it is just a challenge that you can overcome if you chose. With fear in your heart, you will only see the worst there is in people and in life. But with love, your mind will find the best in people, and an attitude of love can bring out the best in people as well.

Choosing again

At some point in your life, you made a choice, usually unconsciously, to either live with fear or love. This decision was most likely influenced by many different instances that occurred in your childhood and affected you profoundly. Regardless, you made a decision, at some point, to hold on to these fears. But just because you made that unconscious decision in the past doesn't mean you have to stick to it in your future. You can choose, and this time, you can choose to feel love and trust in goodness again. When you choose love, you choose to think in such a way that benefits you the most. You are not afraid to be confident because you know that you can do it. You are not afraid to love because you know you will be loved in return. You are not afraid to go out there because you know that your efforts are done in good faith and that you will be appreciated. Loving yourself will allow you to have enough confidence and trust in yourself to no longer fear for the future. You know you will pull through, you know you are capable.

Living with love is making the choice to see the world in the light of goodness, compassion, peace, and hope, which you can also spread to other people around you.

PRINCIPLE 46

HOW TO HAVE A LASTING RELATIONSHIP

Love is an everlasting theme in human life; from biblical times, to the renaissance, up until the present day, love is a huge part of the human story. But finding and keeping love can be very difficult for many people, which is why marriage counseling and dating websites are so popular nowadays. But it is often the little things that keep love alive and strong, little gestures of love can have more impact than all the counseling and trust exercises you end up doing.

Simple loving gestures

Do you tell your partner you love them? Do you remind them of it as much as possible through words and deeds, or do you spend the day just going through the motions because you're already used to each other's presence? Research has shown that couples who still make an effort at romance, no matter how small, tend to last. Telling your partner you love them, saying thank you, or by giving them small tokens of appreciation can go a long way. Always be appreciative of them and their efforts. You can even try to do something special now and then. You can cook them a fancy dinner, do some chores that your partner usually does for you, or take them out to dinner. These may be small gestures, but these can keep the love and romance alive in your relationship, no matter how long you and your partner have been together.

Share with them

Nothing can strengthen a relationship like sharing yourselves with each other. The stress and difficulties you are facing at work or in your other familial relationships can become easier to deal with when you share these problems with the person you are most intimate with. There are those who reason that they don't want to bring their spouse or partner involved in their mess of problems, but isn't that what a relationship is about? And your spouse might welcome the fact that you trust them enough to share your problems with them.

Along with this sharing of present problems, there must be a sharing of the past. The more you reveal yourself to your partner, the easier it will be for them to understand you. As much as possible, do not keep secrets from one other. In order to truly trust and be trusted, you have to give yourself to them and share your secrets. If they don't like it, then it's their loss, but never think that you can hold on to someone and have a real, meaningful connection when your relationship is based on deception and withheld information.

Give time for each other

Spending time with each other is an important aspect of keeping the love alive. Spending time with each other doesn't just mean living in the same house. You have to spend QUALITY time together. Find an activity that you both enjoy, or simply stay at home and have a nice talk, just make sure to give your partner all of your attention. Don't think about work, or bills, or even your kids for the next hour. Focus on each other.

PRINCIPLE 47

LOVE YOURSELF

When seeking success in anything, whether it is personal, professional, or romantic, it is important to have confidence in yourself. Having high self-esteem is what will drive you to work hard and take risks, to be assertive, and stand up for yourself, which is why it is a big part of success.

Everyone has value

There is a basic principle that everyone has the same fundamental, unchanging, and incalculable value just for being who they are. This intrinsic worth is not lessened by other people's view of you, the mistakes you make, or the wealth that you accumulate (or don't). This is the basic foundations for equality, which is to say that everyone has the same worth, the same rights as everyone else, with no regard for race, creed, wealth, or politics.

This principle of equal worth has long been established and even if everyone agrees with it in theory, the truth is that people are constantly being judged and devalued. Especially now, with the advent of social media platforms that allow everyone to broadcast their lives, and open for everyone to judge and criticize, the meaning of self-worth has become subjective.

Why it's destructive to measure your worth with external factors

External factors mean anything and everything outside of your own self, such as other people's opinions, your reputation, your status, your wealth, and other material possessions that people often equate with value and worth. These are things that can add shine or fluff to who you are, but these can never define you. Your intrinsic value and worth as a human being can never be touched or altered by anything external to you. Measuring your value through external things, such as your bank account or professional standing means that your sense of worth and self-esteem can rise and fall according to the amount of money you acquire or your particular performance at work. This way of thinking makes you more susceptible to bouts of depression and self-loathing if it happens that you don't reach your short-term projections. Constantly trying to prove your worth through accomplishments can turn into a very stressful lifestyle.

Be aware of your own worth

But for you to be successful, you have to be aware of your worth as a person, without any of the pomp and vain displays that people often use to measure worth. External ideas, objects, and views cannot diminish your worth as a person, and you have to value yourself, even if you think others do not. As long as you hold a strong and unshakable belief in your own self-worth, you will find yourself to be more confident and assertive, you will truly become a stable and healthy minded go-getter while firmly holding on to your values and principles.

Having a sense and appreciation of self-worth means you can live with dignity and strength of character because you do not measure who you are through the perceptions of others. With this empowering thought, you can finally reach your goals without doubting yourself.

"When you step out of your comfort zone another zone is In-stantly created."

> "PEOPLE LARGELY FAIL TO END UP WHERE THEY WISH TO BE FOR TWO REASONS: THEY HAVE NO IDEA WHERE THEY'RE GOING AND THEY DON'T DO THE THINGS EACH DAY THAT WILL CREATE THE LIFE THEY WANT."

PRINCIPLE 48

BEING AT PEACE

Being at peace is, oftentimes, the most sought after of human conditions. But, it is also one of the most difficult to achieve. People struggle and are face different challenges every day, from struggling with traffic, to struggling with work, to struggling to get the kids to bed, and at times like this, peace seems like a nice but unattainable concept. But there is a way for you to find peace in your life despite the struggles and turmoil that is happening around you.

Stop struggling against yourself

Being at peace also means stopping the struggle against yourself. When you struggle with your weight, your body image, your lack of control, or other negative emotions, you will never find peace in yourself. To find peace, you have to appreciate yourself first. You have to learn to love yourself. This does not mean that you don't try to improve yourself, you still can. You just have to make sure that the improvements you want to make are based on positive and loving feelings toward yourself, not hate or shame. Stop struggling or punishing yourself. Instead, build yourself and improve your health because you believe that you are worth working hard for. But before doing this, you first have to see the beauty in yourself. The same goes for your emotions, your circumstances, and your choices. Accept what is with an open heart and you will surely find peace.

Keep your eye on the present

Continuously agonizing over the past or worrying for the future will keep your life in turmoil. You have to keep your mind on the present and be at peace. Turmoil only comes when you look back on or anticipate pain. Instead, be at peace with the present. In this sense, you can even be at peace with the pain of the present, whether it is physical or otherwise. Let whatever emotion or pain you feel roll through you, be accepting of the pain and it will pass. The more you grit your teeth and deny the pain, or despair over it, the more painful it becomes. Your denial and reactions is hurting you, as well as the actual pain, and you end up subjecting yourself to twofold of the suffering.

Learn to trust and have faith

The universe is wondrous and full of mysteries that we are yet to unravel, and although it doesn't seem like it most of the time, there is order, there is peace in the midst of what seems like chaos. The universe has absolute laws that govern the movement of all things, from celestial object to tiny dust particles. In order to be at peace with life and the universe in general, you have to have faith. This concept doesn't have to follow a certain religion, although it's perfectly fine if you do. Faith simply means that you don't despair or lose hope because of how random things can seem. Have faith that things will be alright, that you'll find a way to get through whatever you're going through. Trust in the universe, for you might not understand it yet, but you have a purpose and there is a plan for you.

PRINCIPLE 49

EMPOWERING THE WORLD

Empowerment means being the author of your own life, being able to take the reins and lead. There are so many people alive today who feel like they have no say in the course of their lives. They feel like little boats being tossed and turned in the giant waves of life, with no sails or oars to help them in their way. It is easy to feel lost and helpless nowadays, but it doesn't have to be the same for you. You can take charge of your own life and empower yourself, and this article will show you how.

Make sure you have your basic human needs

Before you can start thinking about becoming the master of your own life, you have to be master of your basic needs. What are these needs? Food, shelter, clothes and a decent job. There is no way that you can take control of your life without fulfilling these basic needs first. If you find that you are missing one of these, then you will need to ask for help from the government or from your family. Other than these, you need to make sure you have plenty of sleep and you have to have some social interaction as well. You need to be a well-rounded human being before you can think about being in control at any point in your life.

Get into the right mindset

You have to remember that everything in life is a choice, everything. How you feel, how you choose to act, how you respond to stress etc., all of this is a day-to day choice that you can make. You can choose to live in the present, you can choose to live mindfully, you can choose to search for true happiness, and it is all on you. Realize that you are never truly helpless, that you can always make a choice NOT to be the victim. Get into the mindset of positive actions. Start something new or learn something new. Continue to improve yourself. All your efforts towards this goal will help you get into the needed mindset of empowerment.

Make short-term and long-term goals

Know where you want to be in life and what you really want to do, and then make a list of your short-term and long-term goals. You should start with something simple that is relatively easy to achieve, such as jogging for 10 minutes every day, and slowly building them up with goals such as getting a promotion in 6 months, or saving enough for a new car in six months. Make sure that your goals are clear and that you have a plan on how to achieve them. By setting your goals straight, you can then work to achieve them in a well thought-out manner.

Taking control of your own life is not going to be easy. There will be hurdles along the way. If you are committed to making a difference in yourself, you have to be willing to take action and take on the world if needed.

PRINCIPLE 50

LIVE LIFE TO THE FULLEST

Life can be scary. Many people entering adulthood don't really know what to do with their lives, and many in their sunset years look back with a feeling of emptiness in their guts, because they don't really know what they've done with their lives. Life may seem fleeting, but it also offers a wondrous opportunity that not many people ever make much use of: to truly LIVE.

No one can be alive forever, which makes life even dearer. You have to grab this opportunity of life and live your life to the fullest. Go through your years with a thirst to live and take on the world with vivacity and you will have lived a full life.

Do what you want to do

Live your life according to your own standards and do what makes you happy. As long as you are not hurting anyone, you have every right to pursue your own happiness. Don't subject yourself to the opinions of others or what society thinks should be the ideal lifestyle. Shut out all the hate, discouragement, and criticisms of others. Instead, live a life that you know you can be proud of and you are happy with. If you pursue your own happiness, you will find that life happens around you.

Live your life outside of yourself

So many people go to school, graduate, get jobs, buy a house, start a family, and before they know it, it's over. You can go beyond this. You can live beyond your simple, basic needs and choose to affect change with the people around you, and even for those who are far away. Living your life for a greater cause adds so much value to your life that it cannot be replaced by material gain. Live your life adhering to the values and principles that you believe in; don't compromise them for some temporary gain. Living simply but with strong values, pride, and self-respect is so much more important than doing something you don't really believe in for the rest of your life.

Don't be afraid to DO IT

When you have dreams, don't think twice. If it's something that you love and feel passionate about, then why not do it. Don't mind what others think or say behind your back. Do not let fear come between you and your passions. If you truly love to do something, it becomes its own reward, and it is these things that make life truly worth living. Pursue your passions and your dreams. The pursuit itself will be worth it.

Don't allow yourself to be boxed in with what society considers acceptable, or what other people in your life want for you. You have to figure out what you truly want to do with your life. Make sure that it is a passion, that it is something that ignites a burning fire in you. Find true love and follow your dreams. Don't compromise this because it is life after all that you end up compromising.

ONE LAST MESSAGE

"We are what we repeatedly do. Excellence, therefore, is not an act but a habit" — Aristotle

If we're honest with ourselves, this quote will resonate within. We are most known by what we do, not what we say. If we are consistent in our actions and our work ethic, people take notice. Success is a measure of doing the common things uncommonly well. Don't do a good job, do a great job!

By following these principles, you should have no issues in increasing to your next level in LIFE and moving your way up in the success ladder. Consistently successful behavior translates to excellence. Truly successful people have integrity, a strong work ethic, a desire to succeed and the tenacity to keep working and to keep learning even when things aren't going well. They don't give up easily; they keep moving forward, regardless of how many times they're knocked back.

I have been through some incredible life events. I have had great success and more than a few failures with my dreams and projects. The principles for LIFE in this book are the lessons that I have learned and adapted in my life to help me succeed. I believe that the true success is not achieving the end result but the journey to achieving that success. What you learn and who you become on the way is the true to success.

Two things I have learn on my way and I believe we can agree on, you miss all the shots you don't take and there is no traffic at the top of the freeway to greatness.

Make sure to always be honest with yourself. Work hard. Don't give up. Be consistent and persistent. Do a great job with everything you commit to and enter every commitment with success on your mind.

Don't wait for success to come to you. Be proactive to ensure that you attain the success you desire. Take the initiative to do more than is expected of you each day. Be excellent in your work. Then, when the opportunity presents itself, make the most of it. Ask yourself every day, "Am I consistent in my actions? Do I do my best work each and every day? Am I providing my commitment to excellence rather than mediocrity? Am I doing more than is expected?" If you can answer yes to all those questions, you are truly "Starting With YOU in LIFE".

Remember, Don't ever stop investing into your continued education with personal development. You must always continue raising your personal development level so you can continue raising your success level. Never expect your success level to be at a 7 to 8 while your personal development level is at a level of 4 or 5.

I live by a motto and that is to always to Inspire, Motivate and Empower others and by doing so I believe that success will manifest within my life. So I encourage that you to do the same and pay it forward by passing along a copy of this book to your friends and family so you can help to make a positive difference in their lives and you too can manifest success within your life by blessing others.

Thank you again for reading this book. Make sure to read it a couple more times until these principles become second nature.

Mike Driggers

ABOUT THE AUTHOR

Mike Driggers Is a Top selling author, International in demand celebrity speaker, the world's leading Authority Marketing Agent, consultant, business owner and master strategist who inspires, motivates, and empowers people worldwide. Mike has been featured on ABC, NBC, FOX, CBS, PBS, USA Today, Business Journal, Wall Street Journal and the Brian Tracy Show. Mike is recognized as one of the world's most requested business, sales & marketing consultant. He is an in-demand international celebrity business and motivational keynote speaker who has delivered over 2500 presentations worldwide. Mike consistently wows audiences with his entertaining and interactive keynotes, seminars, workshops, coaching, and training programs.

Mike is the author of several books titled "Mastering of The Mind Set", "Unleash The Intrapreneurship Within", "Nothing in LIFE

Starts Until YOU Start", "Nothing in SALES Starts Until YOU Start" and "Nothing in LEADERSHIP Starts Until YOU Start" "Managing Your Commitment". Mike has also co-authored several books titled "Entrepreneurs On Fire" with Barbara Corcoran from the hit TV series, The Shark Tank, "Reach Your Greatness" with James Malinchak from the featured hit ABC TV Show Secret Millionaire", "On Target Marketing" with Vince Baker co-owner of On Target Marketing Group.

Mike has shared the stage with many great thought leaders like James Malinchak, Brain Tracy, Jon Assaraf, Jack Canfield, Zig Ziglar, Jim Rohn, Les Brown, Loral Langemeier, Rudy Ruettiger, Eric Worre, Jeff Olson, Kevin Harrington, Forbes Riley, Glenn Morshower, Seth Godin, Jill Lublin, Kevin Clayson, Richard Kaye, Joel Comm, Darin Adams, Craig Duswalt, Trish Carr, Berny Dohrmann, Shane Gibson, Seth Greene, David Hancock, Sharon Lechter, Nancy Matthews, Ken McArthur, Nick Nanton, Greg S. Reid, E. Brian Rose, and much more.

Mike has been in the top 10% of producers for the direct sales industry for more than 30 years. Mike has owned and operated several successful businesses, including a Bay Area marketing and advertising agency called Unleashed Media where In 2004, he was voted entrepreneur of the year in his local area by President Bush.

Mike uses a no-nonsense, highly focused and disciplined approach to creating real results quickly. He covers subjects including entrepreneurship, mindset, leadership, sales, marketing, high performance, and motivation. Mike's passion, desire, and willingness to be a servant leader has inspired and helped thousands of people achieve greatness within their personal and business lives. As a consultant, Mike's is a behind-the-scenes, go-to sales, marketing and leadership advisor for many businesses. His clientele is a Who's Who in the fields of sports, business, entertainment, and politics. He has helped people from all walks of life create amazing results quickly and hit top ranks within their business and careers. Vist www.BookMikeToday.com

LET'S MAKE IT HAPPEN TODAY

Special **FREE** Bonus Gift For **YOU!**

To help you stand out from the crowd
FREE BONUS RESOURCE for you at;
www.letsmakeithappentoday.com/sp.html

Get your FREE Report And You'll Discover...

1. How to avoid being like the vast majority of people, having hundreds of projects started and never completed

2. How to choose and write Your goals effectively, how to write effective action plans and how to make sure you stick with your goals and never give up.

3. How to become remarkably effective by fulfilling your Goals and Start Living the Life of Your Dreams

www.letsmakeithappentoday.com/sp.html

THE IDEAL PROFESSIONAL SPEAKER FOR YOUR NEXT EVENT!

Any organization that wants to develop and grow their business to become "extraordinary" needs to hire Mike for a keynote and /or workshop training!

TO CONTACT OR BOOK MIKE TO SPEAK:

IME Publishing Group

(866) 7BOOKME

(866) 726-6563

www.BookMikeToday.com

Info@SuccessWithMikeDriggers.com

Nothing In LIFE Starts Until YOU Start

"Share This Book"

Retail 24.95

Special Quantity Discounts

5-20 Books	21.95
21-99 Books	18.95
100-499 Books	15.95
500-999 Books	10.95
1,000 + Books	8.95

To Order Go To www.BookMikeToday.com

www.ingramcontent.com/pod-product-compliance
Lightning Source LLC
Chambersburg PA
CBHW070816100426
42742CB00012B/2373